LIFEBOAT STATIONS OF NORTH EAST ENGLAND

FROM SUNDERLAND TO THE HUMBER

THROUGH TIME

Paul Chrystal

AMBERLEY PUBLISHING

About the Author

Paul Chrystal is author of more than twenty books. They include the following titles in the Amberley Publishing *Through Time* series: *Knaresborough; North York Moors; Tadcaster; Richmond & Swaledale; Northallerton; Hartlepool; Harrogate; Redcar, Marske & Saltburn; Vale of York; In & Around Pocklington; Barnard Castle & Teesdale; Selby & Goole*, 2012; *Fry & Cadbury Through Time; Confectionery in Yorkshire Through Time; Villages Around York; In & Around York; York Places of Learning; York Industries*, 2012.

Other books by Paul Chrystal: *A Children's History of Harrogate & Knaresborough*, Hometown World, 2011; *A to Z of Knaresborough History Revised Ed*, Amberley Publishing, 2011; *Knaresborough Then & Now*, History Press, 2013; *Women in Ancient Rome*, Amberley Publishing, 2013; *Chocolate: The British Chocolate Industry*, Shire Publishing, 2011; *York Then & Now*, History Press, 2010; *The History of Chocolate in York*, Pen & Sword, 2012; *In & Around Easingwold: The Passage of Time*, GH Smith 2012; *The Rowntree Family*, Amberley Publishing, 2013

To all lifeboat men and women – past, present and future

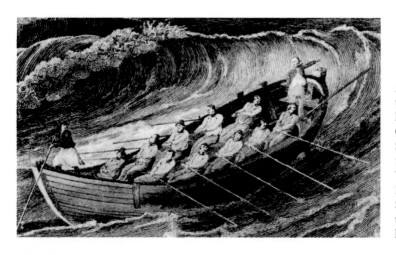

An engraving showing the *Original*, the lifeboat built by Henry Greathead at South Shields, published in 1802 as a 'Perspective View of Mr Greathead's Boat Going to Assist a Ship in Distress'. It was the first purpose built lifeboat.

First published 2012

Amberley Publishing
The Hill, Stroud, Gloucestershire, GL5 4EP
www.amberley-books.com

Copyright © Paul Chrystal, 2012

The right of Paul Chrystal to be identified as the Author of this work has been asserted in accordance with the Copyrights, Designs and Patents Act 1988.

ISBN 978 1 4456 1376 5 (print)
ISBN 978 1 4456 1380 2 (ebook)

British Library Cataloguing in Publication Data.
A catalogue record for this book is available from the British Library.

Typesetting by Amberley Publishing.
Printed in Great Britain.

Preface

The east coast holds the record for the largest number of sea disasters round the shores of the British Isles. This book is the first to describe and depict some of the lifeboat stations and the lifeboat crews there, which have courageously dealt with, and in many cases, mitigated these disasters from 1800 to the present day. Taking in the fourteen stations from Sunderland in the north to the Humber estuary in the south it shows the early histories of the lifeboat stations, lifeboats and crews, and their development over the years. It does this through the use of old photographs juxtaposed with modern equivalents to demonstrate how things have changed over the years, all supported by concise, informative captions.

Along the way we take in Sunderland – the first lifeboat station to be established, in 1800; the terrible *George Elmy* disaster at Seaham; First World War bombardments at Hartlepool and Scarborough; the world's oldest lifeboat – the *Zetland* – at Redcar; the audacious and tenacious women of Runswick Bay; Whitby lifeboat's inland rescue in the Ruswarp floods and the awe inspiring trek to Robin Hood's Bay, hauling the lifeboat through a blizzard; Charles Dickens' admiration for the mariners of Filey; the lighthouses and lifeboat stations of perilous Flamborough; Lawrence of Arabia and his work at Bridlington; the Withernsea crew assisting at the Kegworth plane crash; and the unique way of life of the lifeboat crews living on the edge at Spurn Point. Entwined in this journey is fascinating information on the coastguard service, how self-righting lifeboats work, various lighthouses, the changing methods of launching from man (and woman) power and horsepower to caterpillar tractors, and the development of lifeboats themselves.

A final chapter describes the early development of things inextricably associated with lifeboats and lifeboat stations: basic lifesaving procedures, lifejackets, rocket brigades and the breeches buoy. The book concludes with a schoolgirl's description of the ideal lifeboat man and a first-hand account of the bombardment of Scarborough, which wrecked the coastguard station and damaged the lighthouse.

Paul Chrystal, York, September 2012

Acknowledgements

Many people have been very kind, generous and helpful to me in the compilation of this book; without them it would be significantly inferior. They include, in no particular order, Liz Cook and Isla Reynolds at the RNLI in Poole, who provided a number of the old photographs; Eric Priest in Hartlepool and Edgar Atkinson, Treasurer of the Hartlepool Lifeboat Management Committee; Alan Musgrave in Redcar; Vera Robinson MBE, Redcar; Stan Laundon, photographer extraordinaire, who shot some of the (better) modern photographs in the Hartlepool chapter – see www.stanlaundon.com for lots more; George Colley for permission to use images first published in his *The Sands of Time* and *Yesterday Once More* – two superb books about Hartlepool and West Hartlepool; Dave Cocks at Redcar RNLI, www.redcarlifeboat.org.uk; Fred Brunskill at The Zetland Lifeboat Museum, Redcar; Mark Vesey, Scarborough Maritime Heritage Centre; Karen Snowden at Scarborough Museums Trust; Angela Kale, Scarborough Library and Information Centre for permission to use images in the North Yorkshire County Council Unnetie Digital Archive; Roger Pickles, Joint Curator of Photographs, Whitby Museum and the Whitby Literary and Philosophical Society for permission to use images from the Doran Collection; Norman Kirtlan for providing and allowing me to use pictures from his amazing Sunderland archive; Dave Angus for contributing the images of Seaham – his superb collection can be seen on his website www.east-durham.co.uk; Simon Robson, Helmsman, Flamborough lifeboat station, for permission to quote from his website www.sprobson.f2s.com – a mine of information about the Flamborough station; Robin Lidster for kindly allowing me to use some of his images of the Robin Hood's Bay lifeboat and coastguard stations (www.magiclanternman.com); and the Museum of Hartlepool and Hartlepool Borough Council for permission to use the image of Seaton Carew lifeboat.

Introduction

Human nature dictates that whenever anybody is in peril on the seas, someone will often try to rescue them. It is this innate compassion and selflessness which led to early, uncoordinated and sporadic lifesaving acts, which eventually culminated in the Royal National Lifeboat Institution we know and admire today – an institution independent of government and dependent on voluntary contributions, whose rescue boats are exclusively manned by volunteers.

It all started towards the end of the eighteenth century when the output from the factories powering the Industrial Revolution, and the imports needed to produce that output, led to a dramatic increase in the transportation of cargoes around the coastline of Britain. The wind-powered ships were often at the mercy of atrocious weather and treacherous currents and rocks. The first lifeboat operated at Formby near the port of Liverpool in the 1770s. Before long, increasing losses of ships, cargo and lives inspired ship owners and their insurers to mitigate these losses and it is this, partly commercial concern that led to the construction of the first purpose built life-saving boat at South Shields by Henry Greathead in 1790. In the early 1900s Lloyds of London set up a fund to finance the construction of thirty or so lifeboats around the coast of the British Isles. This resulted in the establishment of a number of much-needed, independent lifeboat stations, some of which were on the north-east coast and within the scope of this book.

It was not until 1823 that Sir William Henry published his *Appeal to the British Nation on the Humanity and Policy of Forming a National Institution for the Preservation of Lives and Property from Shipwreck* leading in the following year to the formation of the Royal National Institution for the Preservation of Life from Shipwreck. Despite initial enthusiasm, the institution was languishing in the doldrums by the late 1840s. Nevertheless, impelled by the loss of twenty lives on a lifeboat, which capsized in the Tyne estuary in 1849, the Duke of Northumberland, First Lord of the Admiralty, took over the presidency of the institution and immediately set about modifying the design of the lifeboats. This led to a new, safer, self-righting boat designed by James Beeching and later adapted by James Peake.

Incidents such as the legendary bravery of Grace and William Darling in September 1838 did much to capture the public imagination and cultivate support for the institution. Unsure whether the lifeboat at North Sunderland (Seahouses) had been launched Grace and her lighthouse keeper father set off in a coble from the Longstone lighthouse on the Farne Islands, towards the wreck of the *Forfarshire*, which had broken in half on Big Harcar, a rocky island. They succeeded in saving eight men and a woman on two 2-mile return trips and Grace became a national celebrity, and was awarded the RNLI Silver Medal for Gallantry.

In 1854 the name of the institution was changed to the Royal National Lifeboat Institution, which absorbed over time most of the independent stations around the coast. By 1895 there were 308 RNLI boats in service with many stations operating two boats (due to the limited range of action of the boats) and some as many as five boats as at Sunderland and Hartlepool.

Today it is estimated that RNLI crews, made up of men and women, have saved nearly 140,000 lives since 1824. In 2010, 53 per cent of launches were to assist leisure craft users, 30 per cent to people where no craft was involved, 9 per cent to fishing or merchant vessels and 8 per cent to other sea users. On average, lifeboats are launched somewhere twenty-four times every day; as this book was going to press there had been thirty-three 'shouts' in the last twenty-four hours. In 2011 there were 8,905 RNLI launches (3,288 in the dark) saving 354 lives and rescuing 7,976 people – an average of 22 every day. The RNLI lifeguards attended 15,625 incidents, saved 84 lives and assisted 17,671 people. The fleet comprises over 330 all-weather and inland lifeboats and 4 hovercraft, all housed in 235 lifeboat stations. Proceeds from this book are going to the RNLI to help them save more lives.

Front cover illustrations: Seaham Lifeboat *George & Mary* and the lifeboat crew with young supporters, built for the 1911 coronation celebrations, with kind permission of Dave Angus. Air Sea Rescue exercise off Hartlepool in 2011, with kind permission of Stan Laundon.

Back cover illustrations: The ladies of Runswick Bay launching the lifeboat, with kind permission of Roger Pickles, joint curator of photographs; Whitby Museum; and the Whitby Literary and Philosophical Society. Redcar lifeboat *Leicester Challenge 3* ready for action.

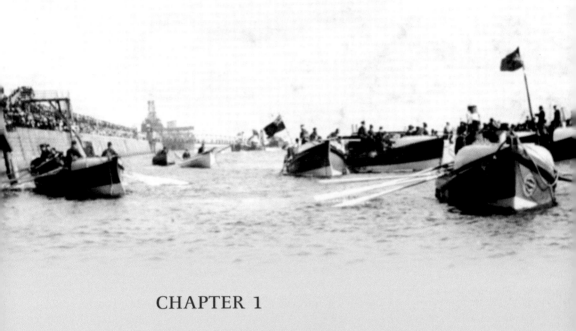

CHAPTER 1

Sunderland

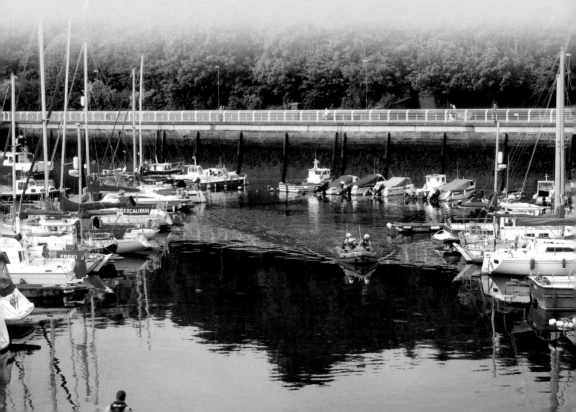

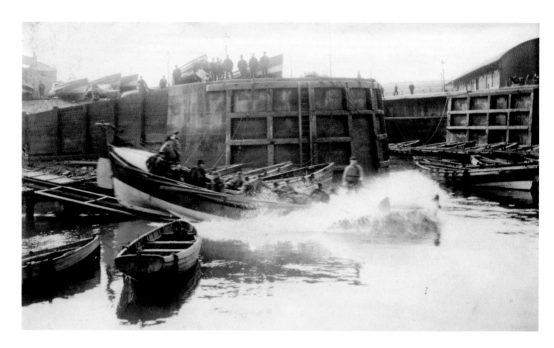

Launch of South Outlet Life Boat

The lifeboat station at Sunderland dates back to 1800. Sixty-five years later it was taken over by the RNLI who provided a lifeboat. It is the oldest continually operated lifeboat station in the United Kingdom. Because of the difficulties finding a suitable site, the lifeboat here has been located at seven different stations; indeed, between 1873 and 1887, Sunderland had four stations simultaneously. The motor lifeboat station from 1912 is the only one remaining. The modern picture shows the *Wolseley*, the current Atlantic class lifeboat.

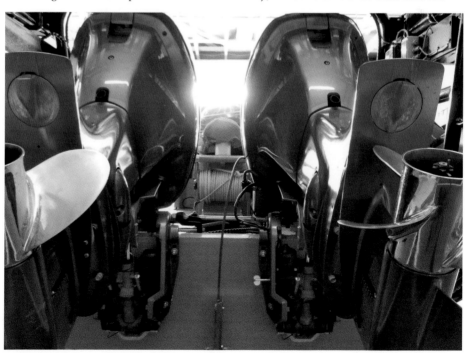

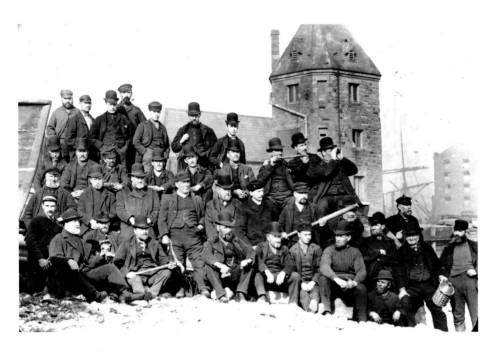

River Weir Harbour Pilots, 1895

A fascinating photograph of the harbour pilots in 1895. In 1856 Joseph Hodgson, a carver, was awarded a silver medal for his twelve years in service, during which he personally rescued ten people from drowning and assisted in saving around seventeen others. The new picture shows crew members washing down after an exercise in August 2012.

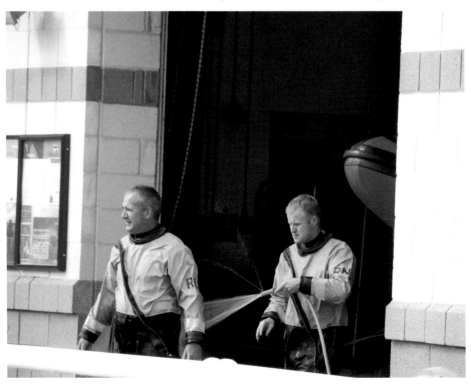

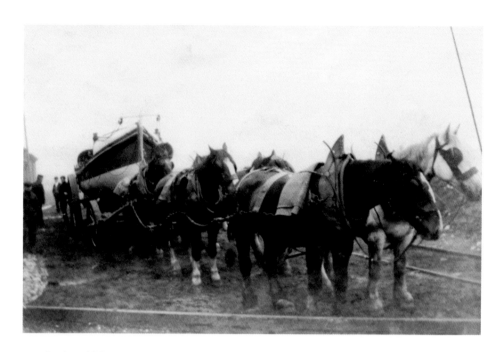

South Pier Lifeboat, *c.* 1908

In 1871 there were two reasonably new lifeboats and a third in the South Dock, with £150 in the bank. Today the station has two lifeboats: an Atlantic 85 Class Inshore, the *Wolseley*, in service since 2007, and a D Class (IB-1) Inshore lifeboat, the *MyJo*, since 2011. The new 2008 boathouse can be seen in the newer photograph along with the 6-metre davit used to lift the boat in and out of the water.

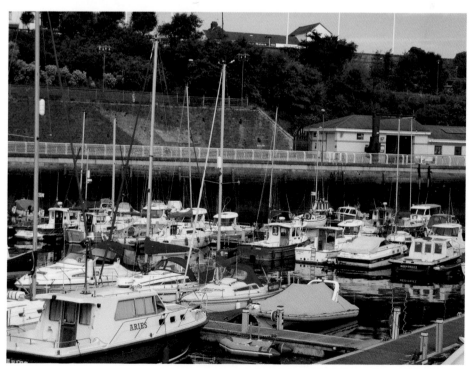

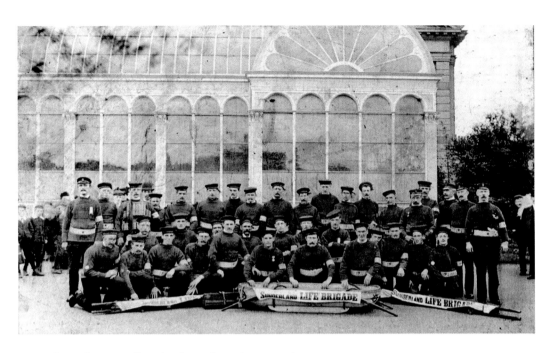

The Volunteer Life Brigade at the Winter Gardens, 1910

Another fascinating picture showing the Volunteer Life Brigade at the Winter Gardens in 1910. The *Good Templar* was a ten-oared self-righting lifeboat paid for by funds raised by the Independent Order of Good Templar's, a temperance organisation founded in Utica, New York, in 1851 and originally known as the Knights of Jericho. A crew change during exercises is displayed in the new photograph, taken in August 2012.

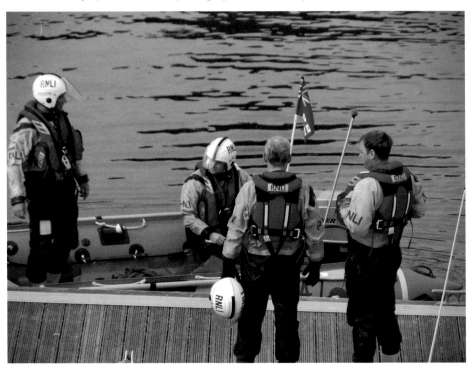

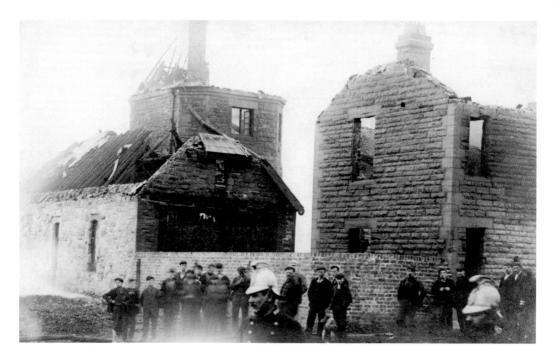

The Lifeboat House Fire, 1882

A gas explosion wrecked the watch house of No. 3 lifeboat house. There were two serious casualties: the coxswain had both legs broken and a Mr Briggs sustained injuries, which resulted in his foot being amputated. The watch house was rebuilt the following year at a cost of £80. The contemporary picture shows RNLI lifeguards preparing the rescue watercraft in the old inland lifeboat station.

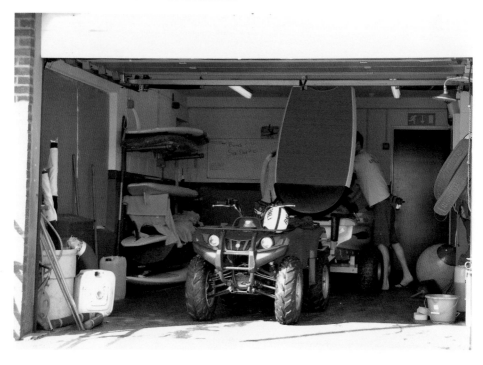

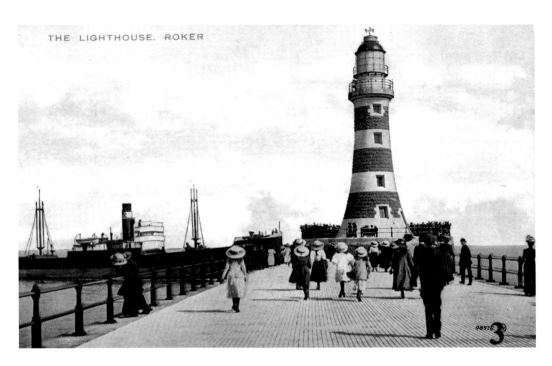

THE LIGHTHOUSE. ROKER

To the Lighthouse
The hullabaloo in the early 1900s was to get a good look at the ship, which crashed into the end of the Roker Pier causing much damage. The other photograph shows the lighthouse today with yachts from the Sunderland yacht club in the foreground.

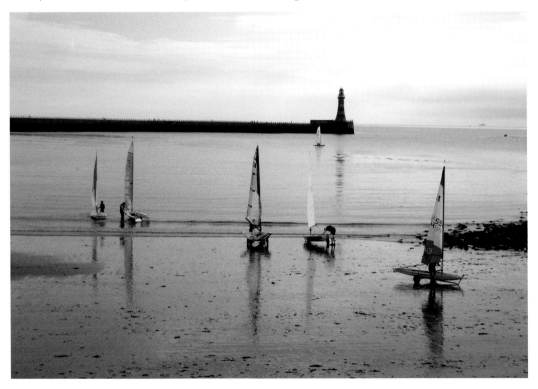

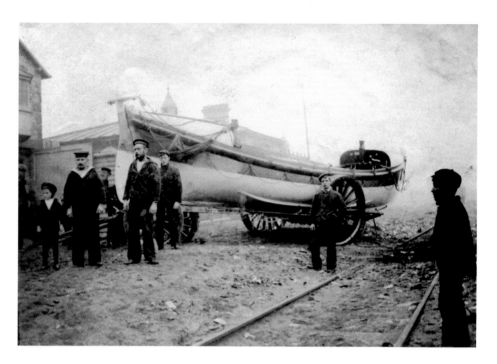

South Pier Lifeboat

In 1895 a new slipway was constructed at South Outlet station. Two years later an additional station was opened at Hendon Beach. That same year a crew received £50 for rescuing eleven people from SS *Jocinth*. In 1899, North Dock and slipway were built at a cost of £1,050. The new picture shows a detail from the call-out boards at the lifeboat station.

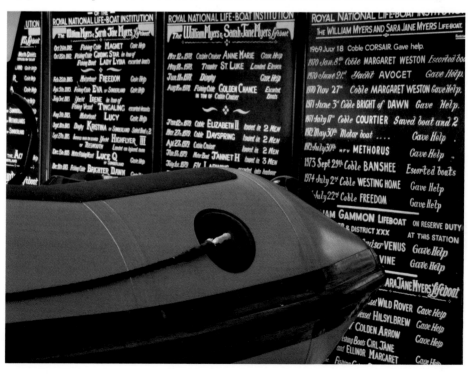

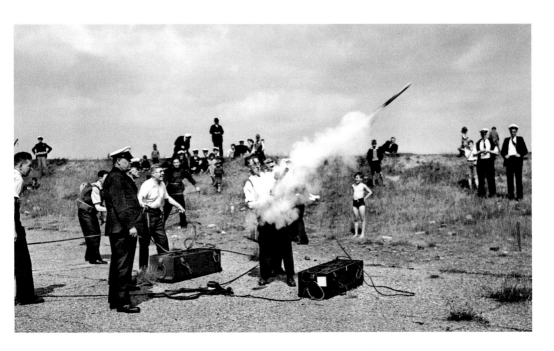

Roker Volunteer Life Brigade Firing Rockets in the Block Yard in the 1950s

South Outlet and Hendon Beach stations closed in 1911. In 1915 a new lifeboat house and slipway were built, costing £2,000. The Volunteer Rocket Brigade originated in the early nineteenth-century with the introduction by Captain George Manby (1765–1854), who lived in Gorleston, of his mortar and rocket-firing rope line apparatus enabling sailors stranded on ships close to shore to be winched to safety. Some contemporary life-saving and safety measures offered by the RNLI are in the newer photograph, taken near to the Sunderland lifeboat station in the marina.

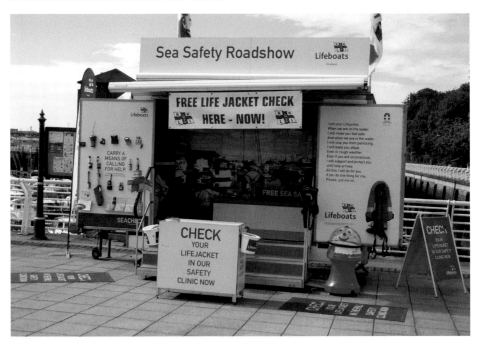

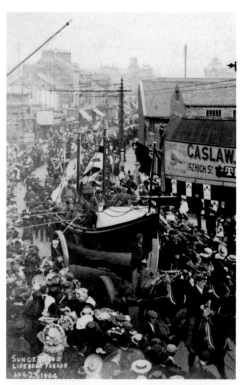

Sunderland Lifeboat Parade, 1904
In 1911 Sunderland's first motor lifeboat, the
1893 *J. McConnell Hussey,* (previously stationed
at Folkestone and Tynemouth) arrived; it was
the first experimental motor lifeboat in the
RNLI fleet.

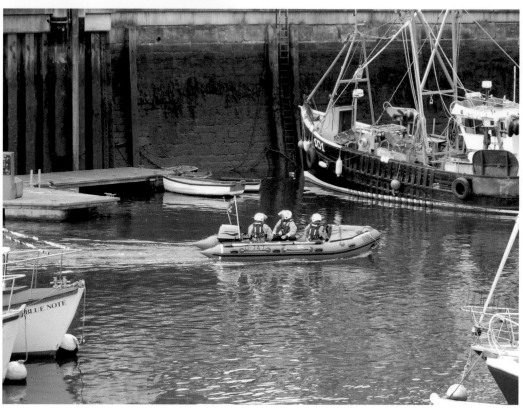

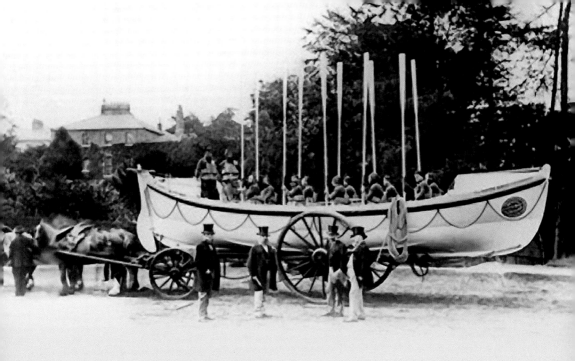

CHAPTER 2

Seaham

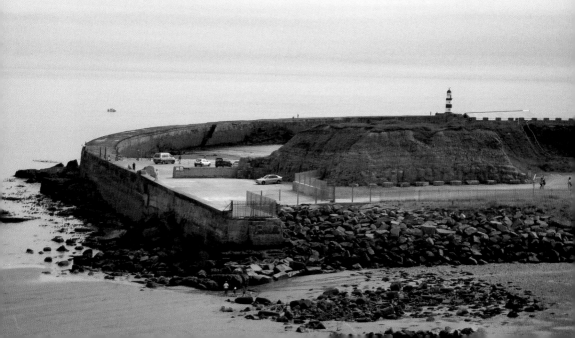

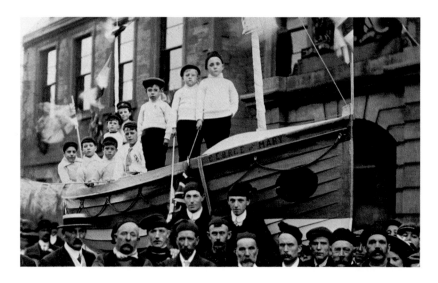

George & Mary

Lifeboat *George & Mary* was built by Coxwain Miller and the lifeboat crew for the 1911 Coronation celebrations. The boys are not known; the lifeboat crew is in foreground. The old photograph on the previous page shows Seaham's first RNLI lifeboat, the *Sisters Carter of Harrogate*, photographed in the grounds of the Royal Chalybeate Spa in Harrogate before arriving in Seaham in 1870. William Grainge in his *Annals of Harrogate & Pannal*, Vol. 2, tells us that it was 'A beautiful lifeboat, built at the cost of the Misses Carter ... 33 feet in length by 8½ feet wide, and rowed ten oars double banked. It possessed the usual valuable properties of self-righting, and self-ejecting water ... The boat was afterwards sent to Seaham in the county of Durham, where a commodious house was erected for it by Earl Vane. This boat has since been the means of saving numbers of mariners from a watery grave.' The new photograph shows the fine monument erected in honour of those who lost their lives in the *George Elmy* disaster in 1962.

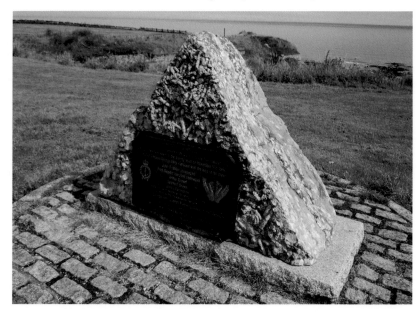

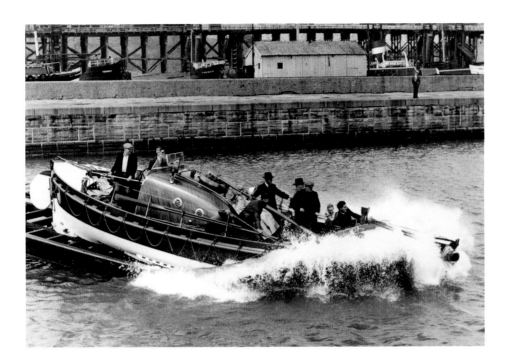

RNLB *George Elmy* and the Restoration Project

The older picture shows the launch of RNLB *George Elmy* just after her arrival in Seaham on 15 January 1950. She was formally christened by the Marchioness of Londonderry later that month. The *George Elmy* was built with the legacy of Miss Elizabeth Elmy, a spinster of Stoke Newington, London, in remembrance of her late brother George. The lifeboat is being restored under the auspices of the George Elmy Heritage (Restoration Project); it was delivered back to Seaham in May 2009. For more information see www.seahamlifeboats.oneuk.com. Work has begun to restore Seaham lifeboat house, which includes a heritage and education centre as well as a dedicated area for the *George Elmy* lifeboat.

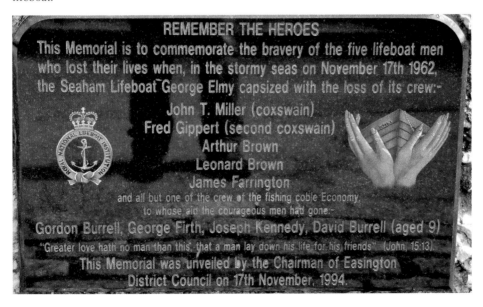

REMEMBER THE HEROES
This Memorial is to commemorate the bravery of the five lifeboat men who lost their lives when, in the stormy seas on November 17th 1962, the Seaham Lifeboat George Elmy capsized with the loss of its crew:-

John T. Miller (coxswain)
Fred Gippert (second coxswain)
Arthur Brown
Leonard Brown
James Farrington
and all but one of the crew of the fishing coble Economy, to whose aid the courageous men had gone:-
Gordon Burrell, George Firth, Joseph Kennedy, David Burrell (aged 9)
"Greater love hath no man than this, that a man lay down his life for his friends" (John, 15:13)
This Memorial was unveiled by the Chairman of Easington District Council on 17th November, 1994.

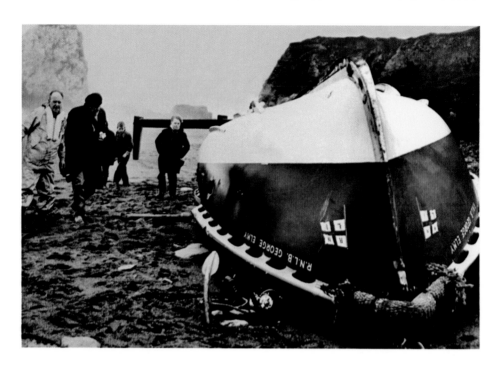

The *George Elmy* Disaster

Two tragic pictures of the RNLB *George Elmy* on Chemical Beach, just off Dawdon colliery, on the morning of Sunday 18 November 1962 after capsizing the night before with the loss of nine lives. Over the previous twelve years *George Elmy* and her crew had responded to twenty-six calls rescuing twenty people before she went to the aid of the fishing coble on that fateful night. She rescued all five on board, but, within a boat length of the South Pier a freak wave capsized the lifeboat and all but one of those on board was lost. The station was closed in 1979.

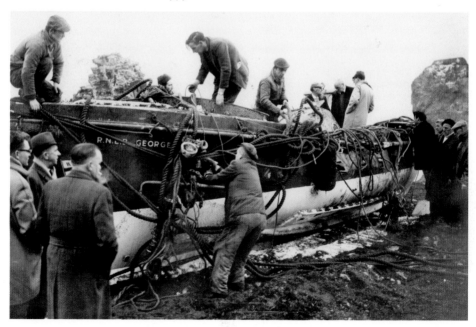

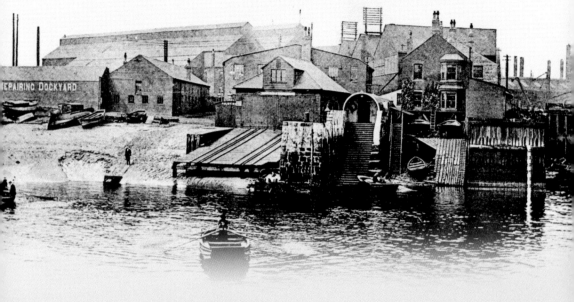

CHAPTER 3

Hartlepool

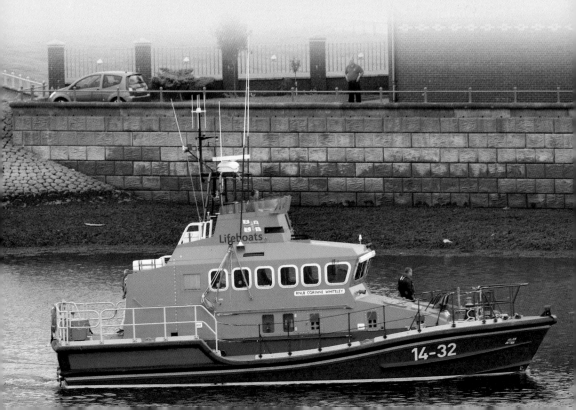

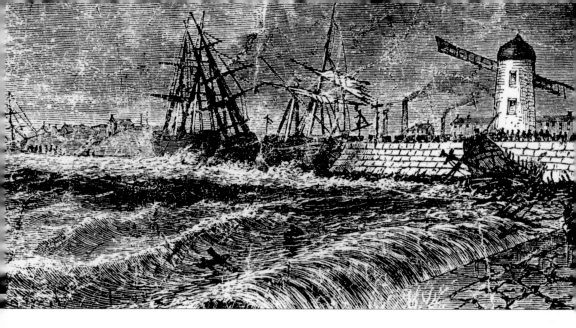

The Great Gale, 8–9 December 1874
The older photograph on page 19 is taken from George Colley's *Yesterday Once More* and clearly shows the 1881 Middleton lifeboat house and the two slipways. A ferry boat can be seen heading for the steps. The new picture on page 19 was taken by Stan Laundon showing the *Corinne Whiteley*. The new picture below, also taken by Stan Laundon, looks towards Teesmouth and is reminiscent of some of the conditions endured in the 1874 Great Gale as depicted in the older image.

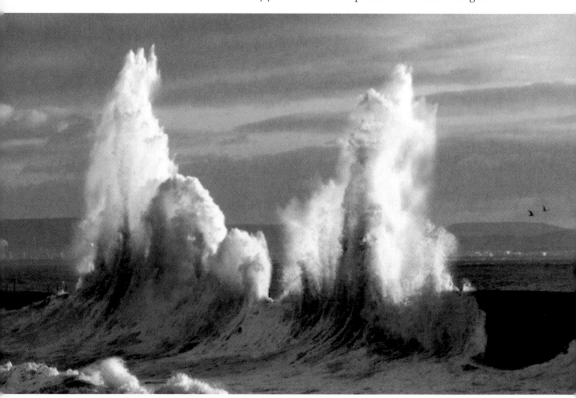

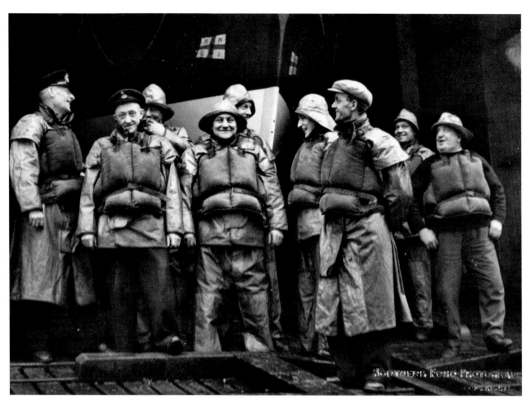

Princess Royal with the 1942 Crew, and the Wreck of the Doris

The nine-man crew of the *Doris*, a Danish schooner, was saved by the *Elizabeth Newton* in 1930 off Longscar Rocks. The *Princess Royal* arrived at Hartlepool on 24 October 1939 to replace the *Elizabeth Newton*; she was a gift from the RNLI, had a crew of 8 and could hold 120 survivors. Her first service was to go to the aid of the trawler *Eileen Wray* that December. In March 1941 she took off the SS *Flimston's* crew of thirty-eight – and the ship's cat – in heavy seas on Longscar rocks. Her last service was in 1968.

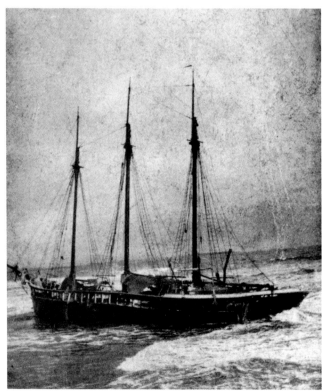

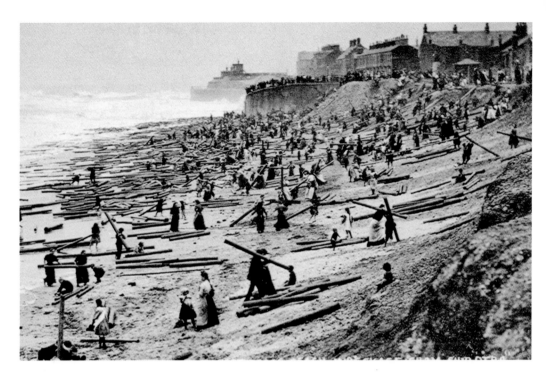

The SS *Otra*

5 June 1912 was a bad night for the SS *Otra*; she was wrecked off the North Sands. This picture shows the unofficial salvage operation in full swing when scores of local residents replenished their firewood stocks from the cargo of pit props conveniently laid out on the beach for them. The new photograph – another of Stan Laundon's – shows a rescue operation off Hartlepool with St Hilda's in the background.

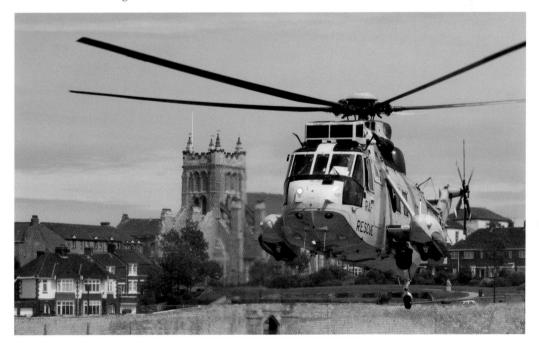

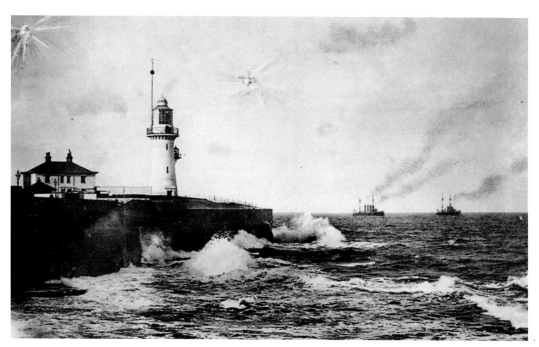

The Heugh Lighthouse 'Under Fire'

The Heugh lighthouse (pronounced *Hyuff*) first shone out in 1847. It could be seen 18 miles away and was one of the first in the country to be lit by gas; the original lantern now resides in the Museum of Hartlepool. After the 1914 bombardment, well under way here, it was dismantled to allow the gun batteries a wider angle of fire. The replacement was built in 1926 and emitted a light equal to 60,000 candles. The card solemnly declares 'For the first time for many centuries the coast of England has been seriously bombarded.' It was originally published years before the bombardment, but retouched in 1914 'to suit the event'. The modern picture shows the lighthouse today, guarded by the Sebastopol Cannon captured from the Russians during the Crimean War, and brought to Hartlepool in 1858.

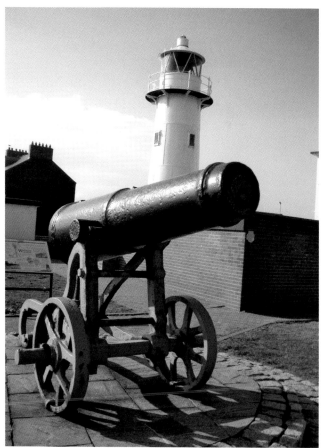

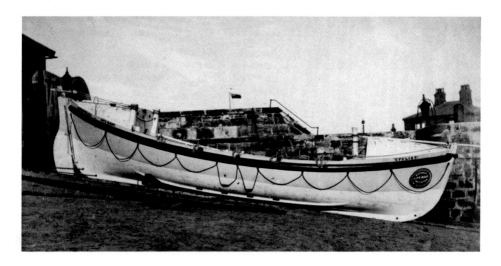

The *Cyclist*

Built in 1887 it served until 1902 and was funded by the RNLI Cyclists' Jubilee Fund in Coventry after a Saturday Lifeboat Day demonstration there, in which a reserve boat from Whitby, the *Joseph Sykes*, was pulled through the city by six horses. The Hartlepool lifeboat story began in 1802 at Castle Eden when, mindful of the great storm of 1785 when thirty-three vessels were wrecked or grounded between Hartlepool and Seaton Carew, it was decided that a lifeboat be built for the Port and Harbour of Hartlepool. The boat began service in 1803. By the 1850s there were lifeboats housed at Sandwell Chare, the Old Pier and at North Sands, two miles north of the Heugh. The obligatory West Hartlepool Harbour and Railway Company boats were at Stranton beach near Newburn Bridge and in the West Harbour. The new photograph shows work going on in Hartlepool port today.

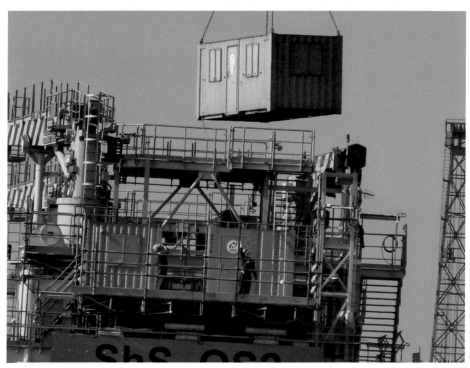

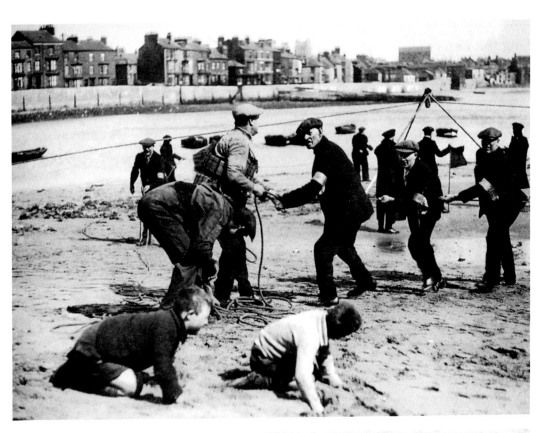

Breeches Buoy Practice 1931 and Team Members

The time-honoured life saving device: a line is shot by rocket to the ship being evacuated either from the shore or from another ship, and secured, usually to the mast. The person being rescued sits in the 'chair', which travels the line to safety. The current lifeboat is the Trent class *Betty Huntbatch*.

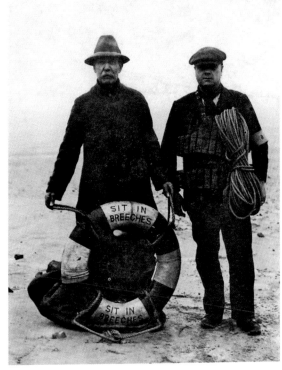

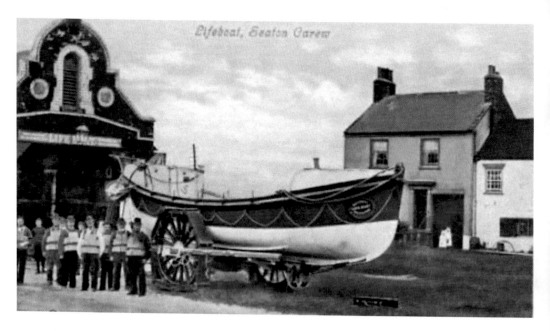

The Lifeboat at Seaton Carew

There were other life-saving stations around Hartlepool. Seaton Carew apart, Blackhall Coast Guard closed in 1975; the crew's cottages were built in the 1850s near the Rocks Hotel and demolished in 1967. Their equipment comprised a cart, a small rescue boat, cliff rescue gear and a large pole for the breeches buoy. In the 1950s the lifeguards shared the beach block in Crimdon with tents, deck chairs, windbreaks, a tea room and the St John's Ambulance Brigade; an extension to house the RNLI lifeboat was built later. West Hartlepool had eight lifeboats between 1847 and 1906.

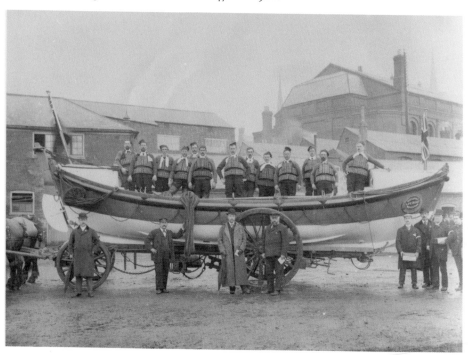

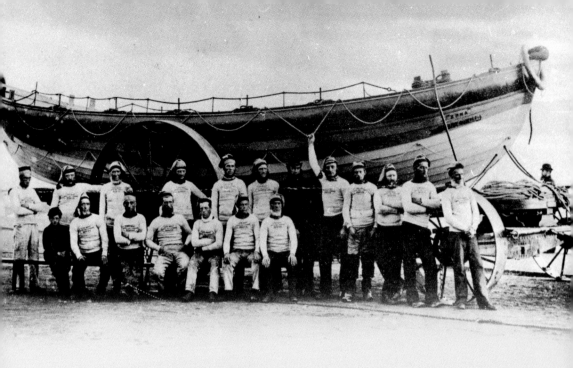

CHAPTER 4

Redcar & Saltburn

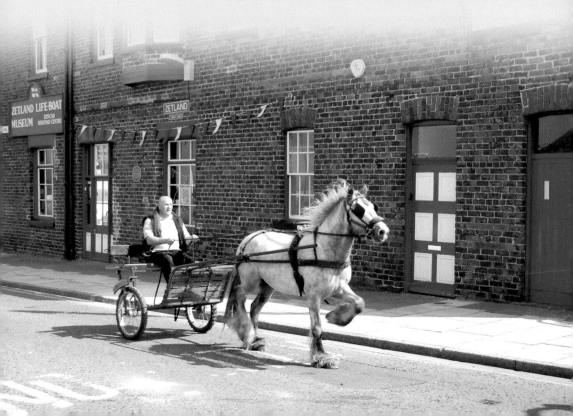

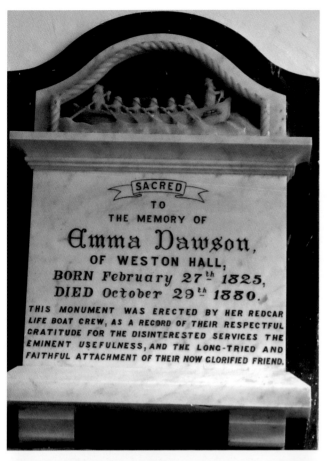

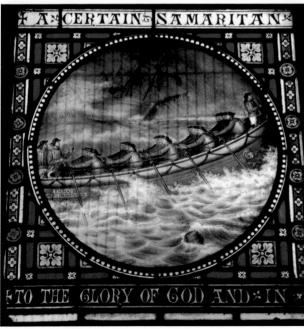

The *Emma Dawson* and the Lifeboat Window at All Saints' Church, Weston

The *Emma Dawson* is the lifeboat on page 27. As can be seen here, it features, unusually, in a window in All Saints' Church in Weston, near Otley. It was commissioned by the National United Order of Free Gardeners to honour Emma Dawson of Weston Hall after she died in 1880. The Redcar lifeboat crew at the time reciprocated by erecting a wall tablet in gratitude for her support. The death of her husband had made Emma Dawson a wealthy widow and a benefactor of some repute. Every Whit Monday she would come to Redcar where she was well known for her generosity and public spiritedness, particularly towards Redcar's fishermen and their families. In 1858 the existing lifeboat, the *Zetland*, was consigned to the scrapheap by the RNLI although, after much local protest, they relented and allowed the townspeople to make repairs and keep her in service. The problem would not go away, however, and the RNLI persisted in their efforts to replace the *Zetland*. Despite this, the Free Gardeners intervened in 1875 to raise money for a new boat, designed along the lines of the *Zetland*, much to the annoyance of the RNLI who had their own designs. A £600 non-RNLI specification boat and a £700 boathouse, with a fishermens' clubhouse above, were duly built with substantial donations from Emma Dawson and Lord Zetland. The launch took place in 1877 before nearly 20,000 people.

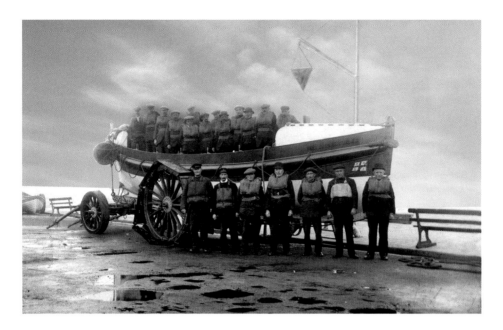

Fifi & Charles

The *Fifi & Charles* saw service between 1907 and 1931, taking over from the *Brothers*. Perhaps her greatest moment came in 1914 when the steamship *Meadowfield* ran aground at Eastscar *en route* from Archangel to London, laden with timber on 10 December. The *Fifi* went to the rescue, manned by a complement of territorial soldiers, as well as the usual crew. With a broken propeller and a leaking hold the *Meadowfield* limped to Hartlepool with the *Fifi* in tow, in case it was needed on the short journey. In 1921 a Redcar woman was crushed to death while helping to launch the *Fifi* to assist the Greek collier, *Aphrodite*, the usual horses being unavailable. The tragedy resulted in the construction of a slipway opposite the lifeboat house. The *Fifi & Charles* was the last of Redcar's rowing lifeboats and was the first to use Redcar's tractor. The new picture shows Redcar's lifeboat station today.

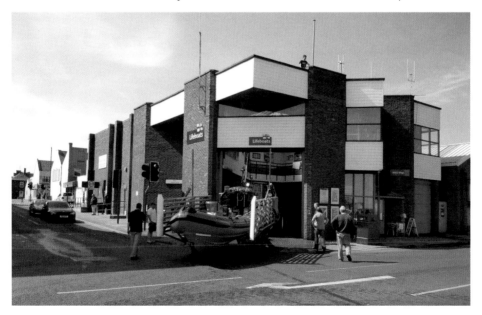

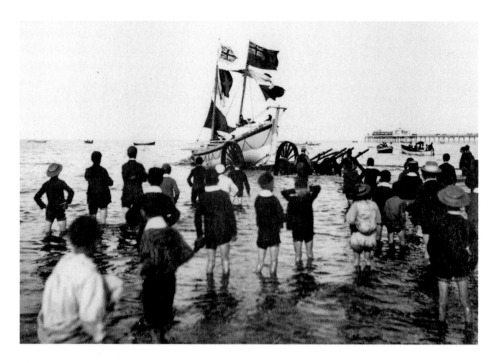

The *Brothers* on Lifeboat Day

Taken around 1885 this picture shows the *Brothers* which was in service here from 1885 to 1893. The pier is in the distance and is virtually complete with the bandstand at the end, although the steamer landing jetty has gone after being damaged by the SS *Cochrane* in 1885; in 1888 the pier was destroyed in a fire. The new picture shows the Atlantic 85 lifeboat *Leicester Challenge 3* ready for action. Redcar's inshore lifeboat is the *Jacky Hunsley*.

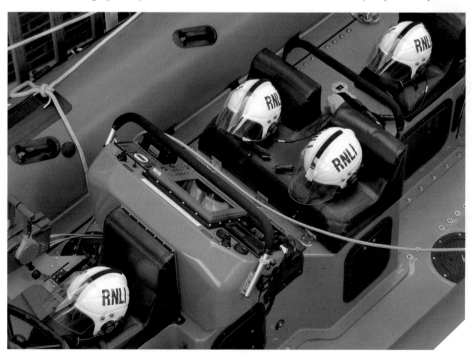

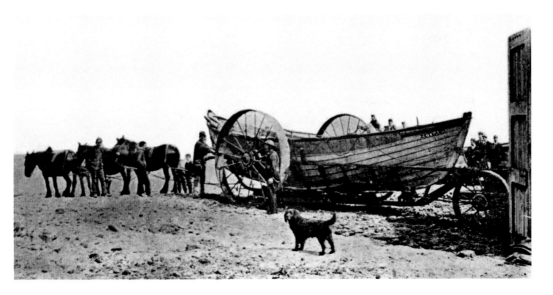

The *Zetland*

The oldest lifeboat in the world, the thirteen-man *Zetland* was built by Henry Greathead in 1802 and was in service for seventy-eight years, during which time she saved over 500 lives, for the loss of one crew member, William Guy, on Christmas Day 1836. Double-ended to obviate the need for turning round, the 30-foot, very shallow, boat was made from English oak and larch, and her gunnels were lined with cork for buoyancy. A local farm provided up to nineteen horses for the launches. After a long and circuitous voyage she now resides, thoroughly restored, in the Zetland Museum in Redcar.

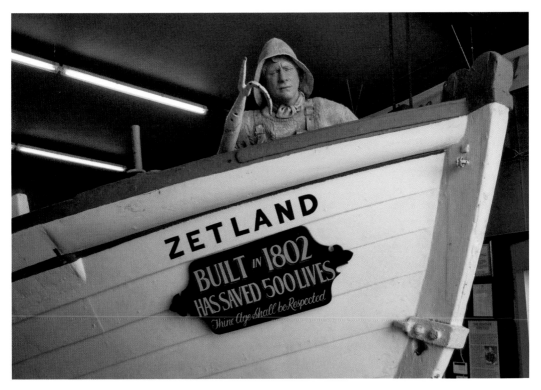

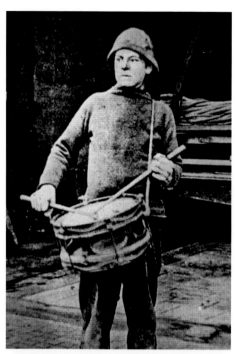

Redcar Drummer Boy

The drummer boy routinely alerted the lifeboat crew with the rhythm 'Come Along, Brave Boys, Come Along'. Down the coast at nearby Skinningrove, the Auxiliary coastguards were made up of men too old for active service or miners and others in reserved occupations; their role was to man the observation posts looking out for U-boats, enemy aircraft dropping mines and drifting mines. They used the local Gas Board wagon to get their equipment to the cliff top.

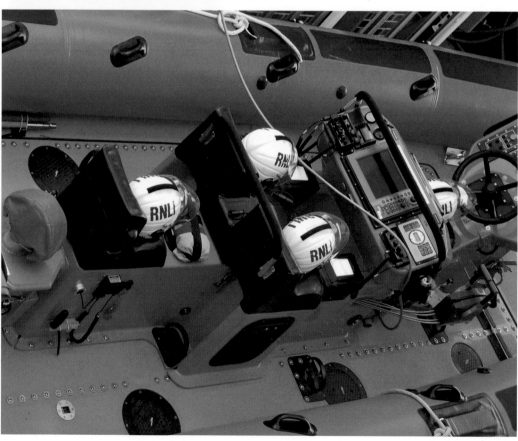

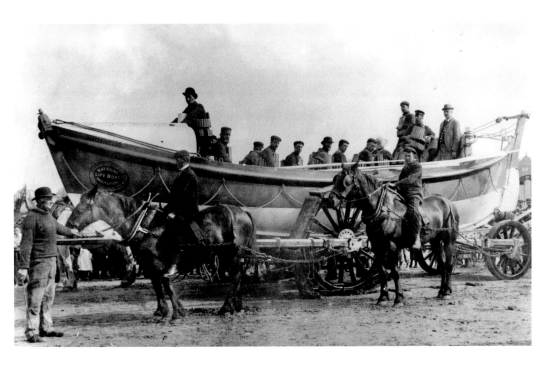

The *Brothers* on the Beach

The *Brothers'* greatest moment came in 1906 when it rescued 114 crew and passengers on the Japanese liner *Awa Maru,* stuck on Westscar on its way to Middlesbrough from Antwerp. The survivors were put up in the Queens and Swan hotels. However, the *Brothers'* back was broken and she was replaced by the *Fifi & Charles*. The new photograph shows the busy Tees estuary today.

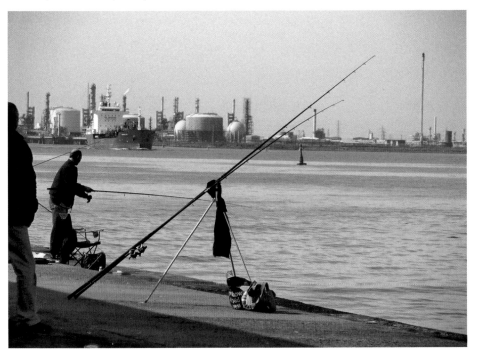

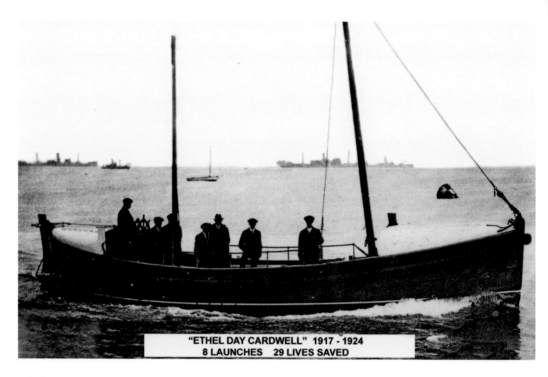

"ETHEL DAY CARDWELL" 1917 - 1924
8 LAUNCHES   29 LIVES SAVED

Ethel Day Cardwell, Teesmouth

Given a favourable wind, the Teesmouth lifeboat crew responded to calls on the last leg to the boathouse on a sail driven bogey running through the dunes on railway lines to South Gare, which still can be seen today. During the 1950s and early 1960s the crew met at Redcar bus station and boarded a special emergency bus for the Gare, sometimes causing considerable inconvenience to the townspeople. (*See page 35.*)

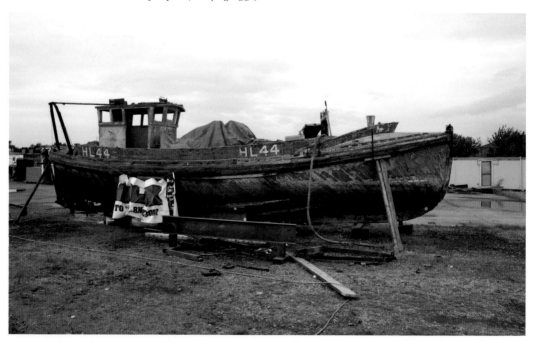

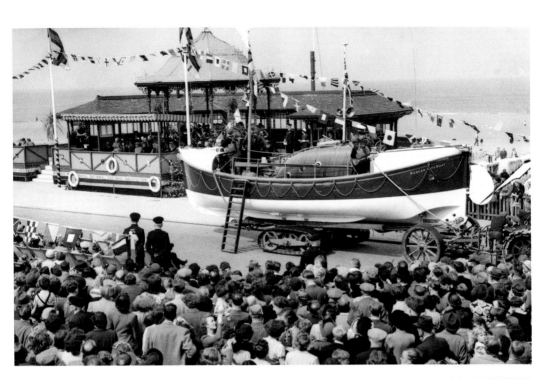

The Naming of the *City of Leeds*

The *City of Leeds* was named by Princess Mary, the Princess Royal, in 1951. She was the first Redcar boat to be fitted with wireless. Her first major service was to assist the Greek steamer *Taxiachia, en route* to Leith from the Black Sea, which had run aground on Westscar after being enveloped in heavy industrial smoke blowing out from the town.

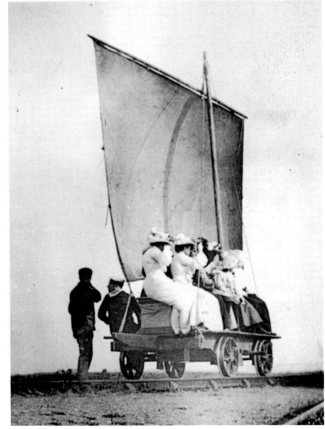

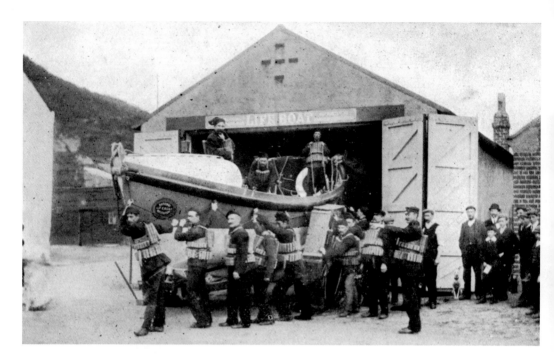

Saltburn Lifeboat *Mary Batger*

The Ship Inn, until 1881, was used as the local mortuary for the many victims of drowning, washed up on the beach here – they were 'accommodated' there awaiting post mortem. A proper mortuary was eventually built by Brotton Local Board; Saltburn Local Board declined to contribute to the cost. The mortuary was one of three buildings on the site. The lifeboat house was nearest to the Ship Inn, while the Rocket Brigade building was between the mortuary and the lifeboat house. Only the mortuary lives on; the lifeboat house and the Rocket Brigade building were demolished when the road was widened. It was not only drowning victims who passed through here; until the early 1970s anyone who died a 'sudden death' was taken to the mortuary on the authority of the Cleveland Coroner.

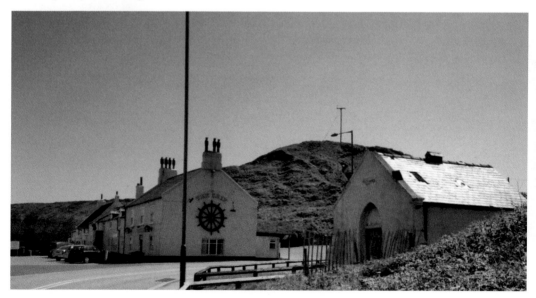

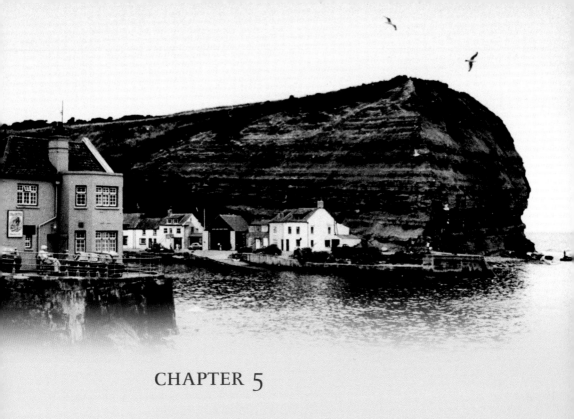

CHAPTER 5

Staithes &
Runswick Bay

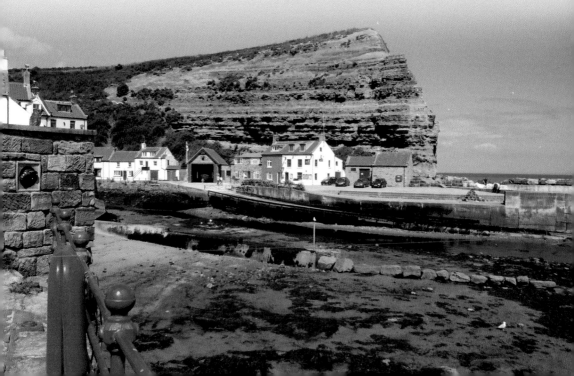

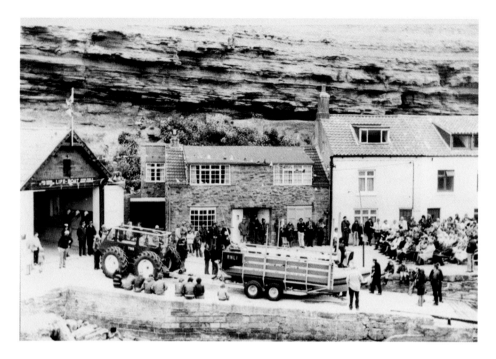

Staithes

The pictures on pages 37 and 38 show the lifeboat station at Staithes built in 1910. The stations at Staithes and Runswick were established in 1874 and 1866 respectively. Staithes Life Saving Company was responsible for rescues from the shore, which mainly involved firing a rocket onto vessels in distress – the forerunners of the Coastguard Auxiliary Service.

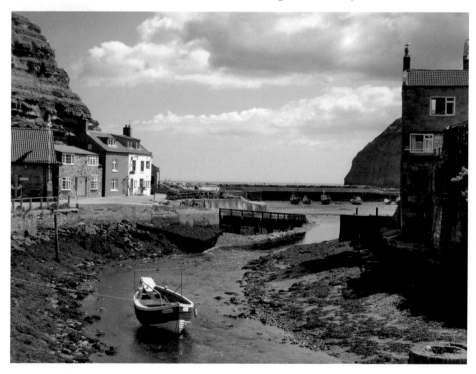

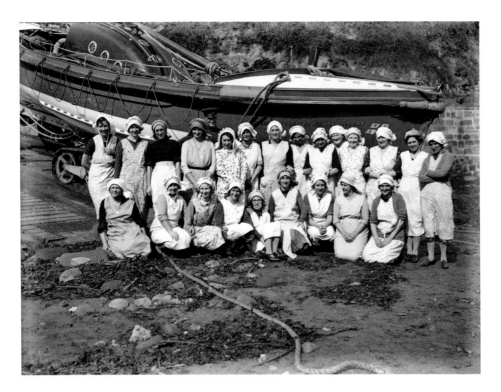

The Women of Runswick Bay

These two fascinating photographs show the women of Runswick Bay launching the *Robert Patton – The Always Ready* in March 1940 to assist the *Buizerd* of Groningen; the six crew were saved. This was not the first time women had helped. On 12 April 1901 most of the able-bodied men were at sea in their cobles when the lifeboat, *Jonathan Stott*, was needed to offer assistance. Only boys and old men remained onshore at the time so the ladies decided that the men and boys would man the vessel and they would launch it. All the cobles returned to shore safely.

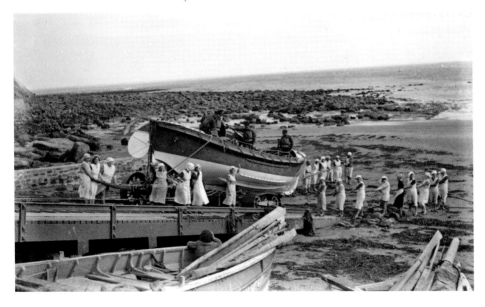

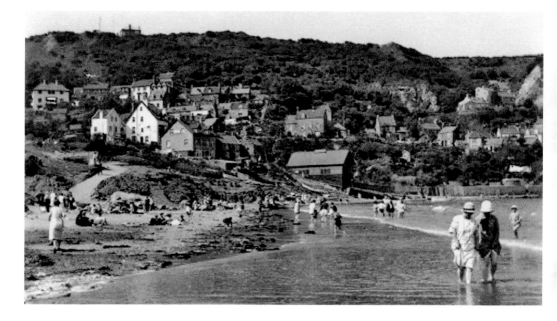

Runswick Bay Rescue Boat

The Runswick Bay lifeboat station closed in 1978 after a number of years when the crew there had to be augmented by men from Staithes to make up the numbers. They were driven to Runswick Bay in a van to join the lifeboat. Eight lifeboats were in service between 1866 and 1978, plus temporary boats. They were launched 203 times and saved an estimated 269 lives. The boathouse can be seen in the centre of the old picture; the new picture shows an exercise off Staithes. The independent Runswick Bay Rescue Boat (currently the *Spirit II*) has operated from the boathouse since 1982, working closely with the RNLI and HM Coastguard. It is dependent on fundraising and manned by volunteers.

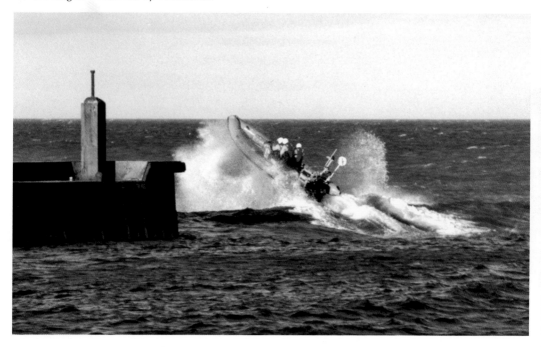

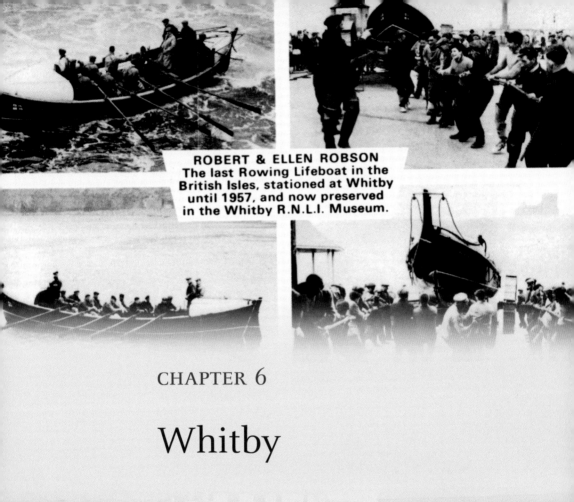

ROBERT & ELLEN ROBSON
The last Rowing Lifeboat in the
British Isles, stationed at Whitby
until 1957, and now preserved
in the Whitby R.N.L.I. Museum.

CHAPTER 6

Whitby

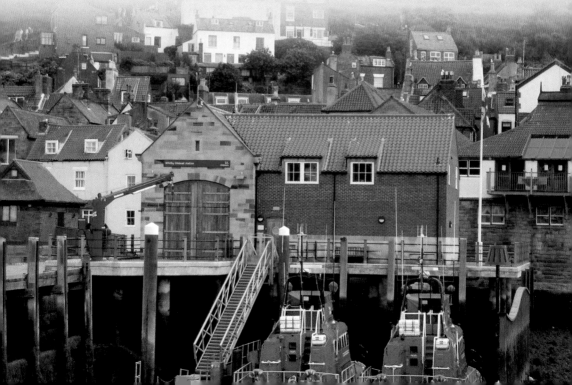

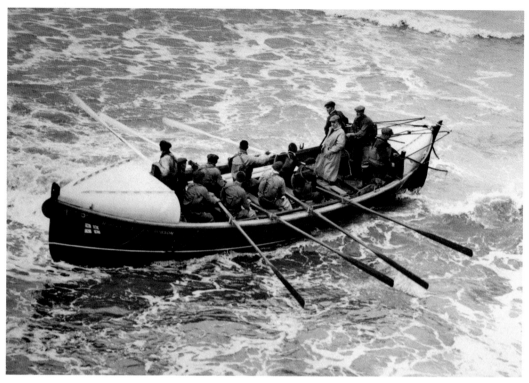

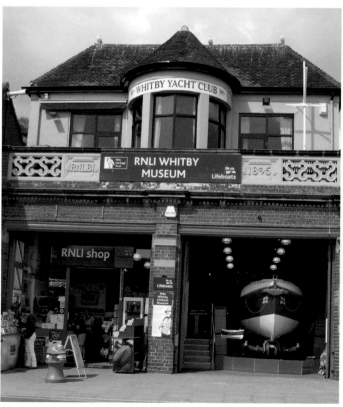

The *Robert & Ellen Robson*
The last rowing lifeboat in the British Isles served between 1947 and '57 with fifteen launches. The Whitby lifeboat story begins in 1802 when Francis Gibbons, the collector of customs at Whitby, took advantage of an offer from Lloyds of London who contributed £50 to the £160 cost of a Greathead lifeboat.
9 February 1861 was a busy and tragic day for the lifeboat. It launched three times before 2.30 p.m, saving all the crew from the *Gamma*, the *Clara* and the *Flora*. However, a fourth service to help the stricken *Merchant* saw twelve fatalities out of the thirteen men on board.

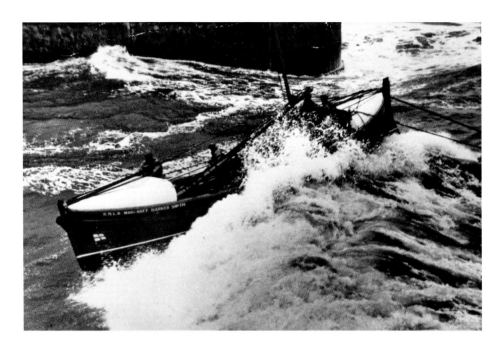

The *Margaret Harker Smith*

Whitby's first motor lifeboat saved eighty-six lives in a service that started in 1919 and ended in 1938, with 117 launches. There was another lifeboat station at Upgang, a mile north of Whitby, which operated for fifty-four years before closing in 1919. Contemporary with the *Margaret Harker Smith* at the Upgang station was the *William Riley*. The new picture shows the Whitby Lifeboat Museum in the old boathouse.

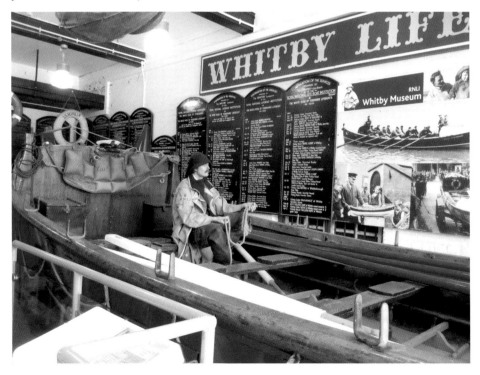

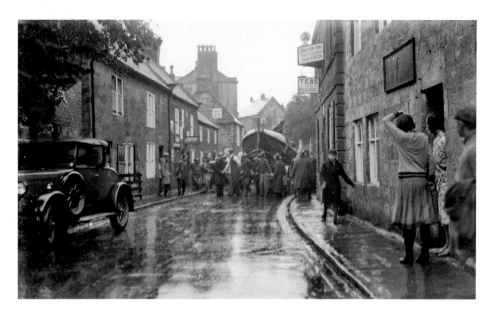

Inland Rescue and the International Flood Rescue Team

The *William Riley* boasts one of the RNLI's more unusual services – 1½ miles inland at Ruswarp. Heavy rains in September 1931 caused flooding with waters over 8 feet deep in places. The village of Ruswarp was particularly badly hit; the lifeboat was hauled to assist there from Whitby by seventy townsfolk. On arrival it was launched into the flood and saved five villagers from their cottages, including a ninety-year-old bedridden lady. Today the 250 strong RNLI Flood Rescue Team, formed in 2000, is available round the clock to deploy to floods in the UK, Ireland and overseas to perform search and rescue. Fifty of the team comprise the international Flood Rescue Team, who can deploy anywhere in the world within twenty-four hours. The entrance to Whitby harbour today (from where Captain James Cooke set sail) with its two lighthouses built in 1831 and 1854 – more illuminated navigational aids than traditional lighthouses – is pictured in the modern photograph.

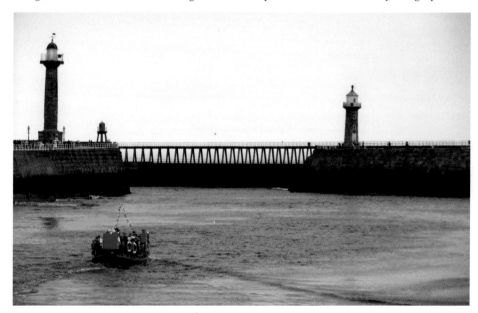

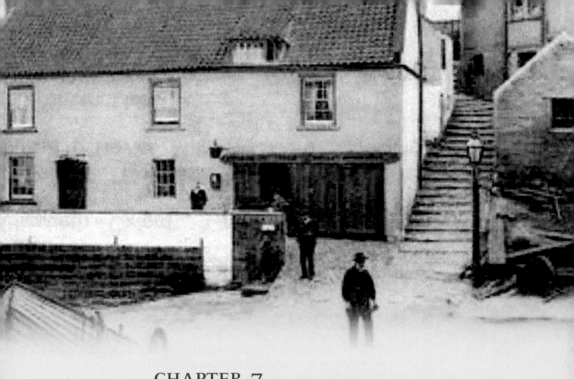

CHAPTER 7

Robin Hood's Bay

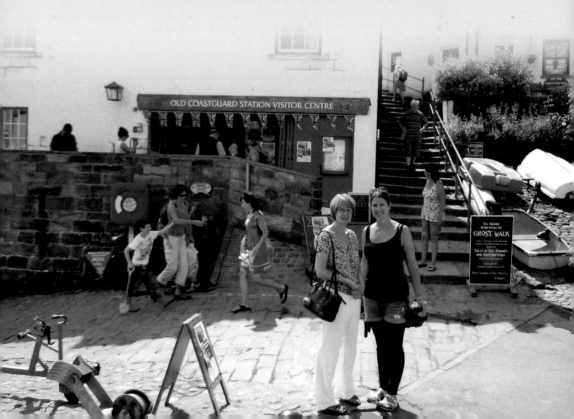

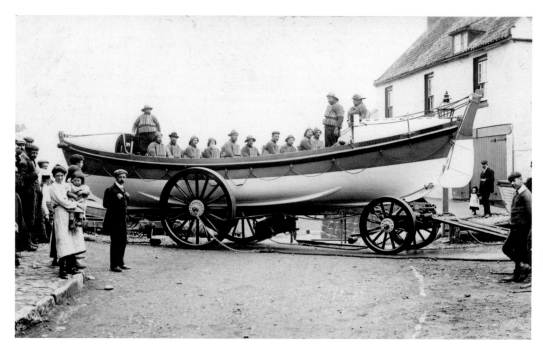

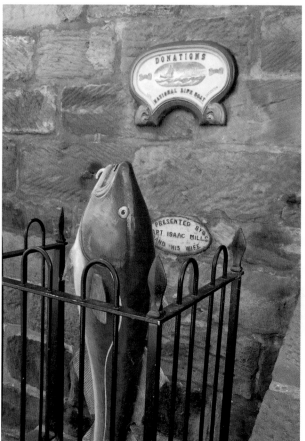

The *Mary Ann Lockwood* (1902–1931)

This splendid card shows the crew outside the lifeboat station at Robin Hood's Bay. The *Mary Ann Lockwood* was the last of four lifeboats here serving from 1830 to the station's closure in 1931. 3 February 1843 was a bad day for Robin Hood's Bay. The lifeboat capsized *en route* to a brig in distress and four crew members died. The coastguard boat was then launched only to capsize with the loss of two further lives out of the five-man crew. The coastguard station is seen in the pictures on page 45, although the newer picture is of the 1960s replica. The signage above the wooden doors in the old picture reads 'Board of Trade Rocket Apparatus'. The coastguards would have kept watch from what was originally a balcony, on the look-out for distressed vessels and smugglers. It is now an information centre. The fish's tail wags (and has done so since 1881) when children feed it with coins.

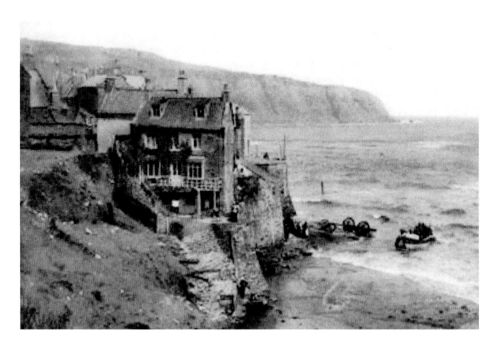

Launching the Lifeboat

The aptly named Oliver Storm was the last lifeboat cox here, coxing the *Mary Ann Lockwood* for its last five years of service. As in Runswick Bay, the women, mainly wives of fishermen, had a key role in local safety at sea. Whenever there was a heavy swell on the landing in the bay – always a bad sign – one woman would go up to the top of the cliff above the village to warn the incoming fishermen by waving a red flag. After dark this was replaced by the glow of an oil lamp strategically placed behind a red blind in the window of a cottage above the ravine.

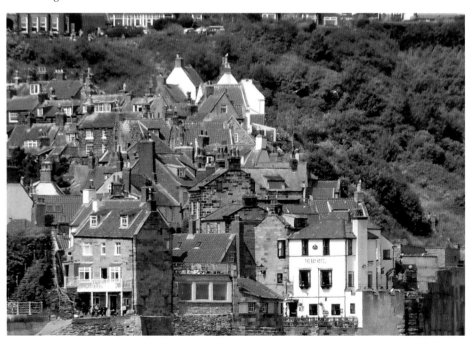

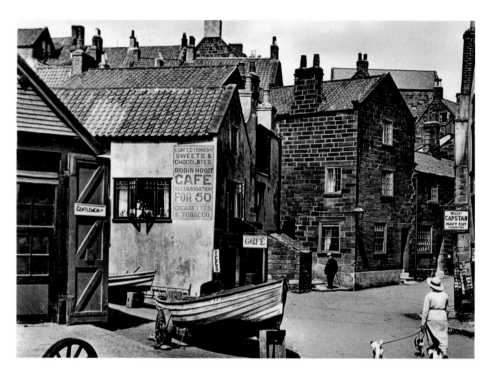

One of the Hardest Launches in History

The boathouse closed in 1931 and was converted into a public toilet. In January 1881 the brig *Visitor* foundered off the bay during a blizzard; the crew took to their boat, but were forced to remain outside the harbour. It was impossible to launch the Whitby lifeboat at Whitby and so 18 horses and around 200 men from Whitby and Robin Hood's Bay hauled the Whitby boat, the *Robert Whitworth*, 6 miles from Whitby to the bay, in snow drifts 7 feet deep in places. At the end of the two-hour trek the men lowered the lifeboat down the steep street towards the seas with ropes. The first launch had to be aborted – the oars were smashed by a wave. At this point John Skelton, a local man with local knowledge of the bay, waded in and swam towards the *Visitor's* crew, plotting a safe route for the lifeboat, now with eighteen crew on board, to follow.

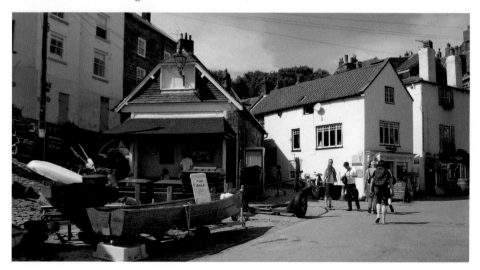

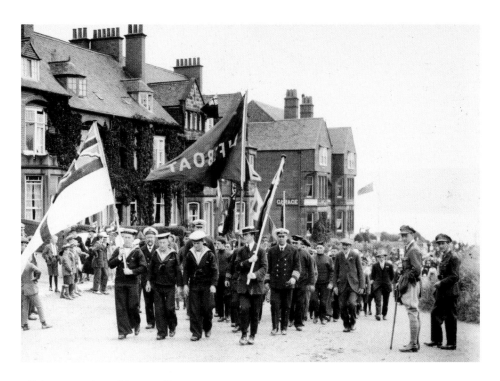

Lifeboat Day in Robin Hood's Bay

Lifeboat Day sometime in the 1930s and the *Mary Ann Lockwood.* Her Majesty's Coastguard is the government service that co-ordinates air-sea rescue, responding to persons in distress at sea, or at risk of injury or death on the cliffs around the United Kingdom. Its predecessor was the Preventative Water Guard established in 1809 to prevent smuggling, but it was also to provide assistance to shipwrecks. Every Water Guard station was issued with a Manby's Mortar. Today the coastguard monitors all maritime distress frequencies and co-ordinates the emergency response, usually requesting the launch of a local RNLI or independent lifeboat, deploying a local coastguard unit, or a search and rescue helicopter.

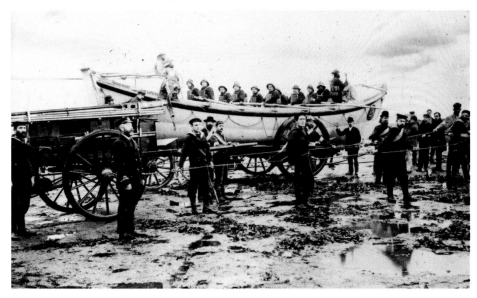

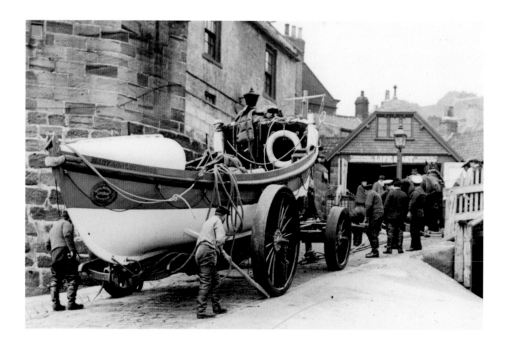

The *Ephram & Hannah Fox*

The old picture is of the *Mary Ann Lockwood.* Note the wedges used by the lifeboat men to prevent the boat rolling backwards should the horses slip. The lifeboat before the *Mary Ann Lockwood* was the *Ephram & Hannah Fox,* which served from 1881 to 1902 with eleven launches saving twenty-four lives. An unnamed boat preceded that with a coastguard rescue boat before that, between 1830 and 1843.

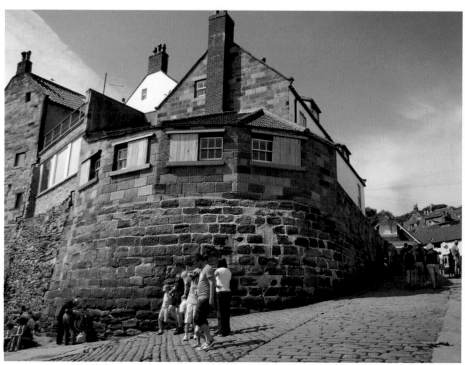

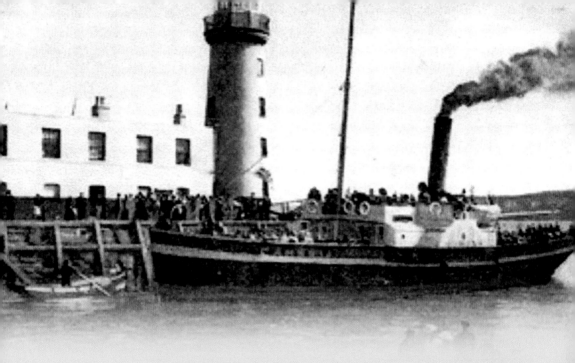

CHAPTER 8

Scarborough

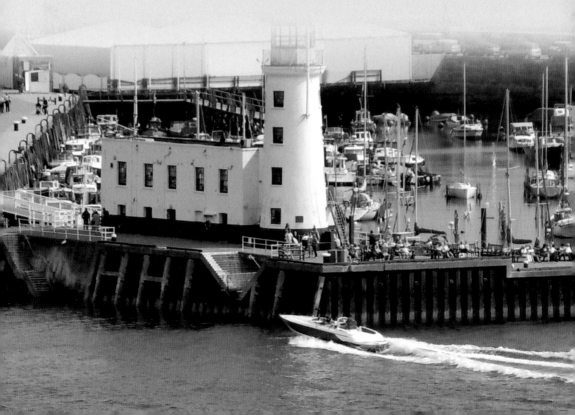

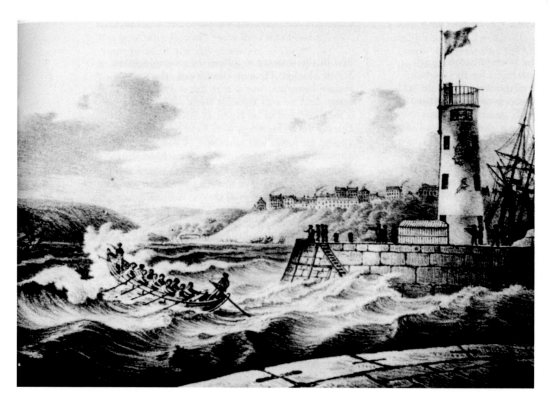

The First *Queensbury* Lifeboat in 1887
The Scarborough *Greathead* lifeboat – Scarborough's first – in 1801 from an engraving by
J. Stubbs. The older picture on page 51 shows the Scarborough lighthouse around 1910.

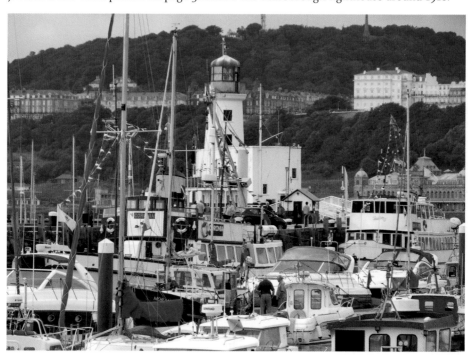

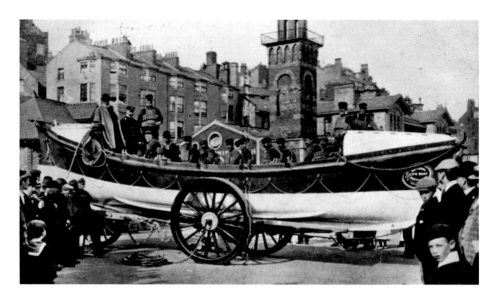

The *Edward & Lucille* (1900–1902)

The first RNLI lifeboat here was the *Amelia*; within two months, however, it was wrecked and replaced by the *Mary*. Remuneration for crews in those days was as follows: five shillings for the crew while on rough weather exercise; three shillings for fine weather exercise; and ten shillings for a service involving the saving of a life or attempts to save life. The *Queensbury* replaced the popular *Lady Leigh* in 1887 and, from the start, was itself very unpopular with the crew. Eight years of protesting to the RNLI finally paid off when *Queensbury I* was replaced with *Queensbury II*, a much lighter, smaller boat, close in performance to the *Lady Leigh*. The new photograph shows RNLI staff setting up for the day in August 2012 with the *Fanny Victoria Wilkinson & Frank Stubbs* in the background.

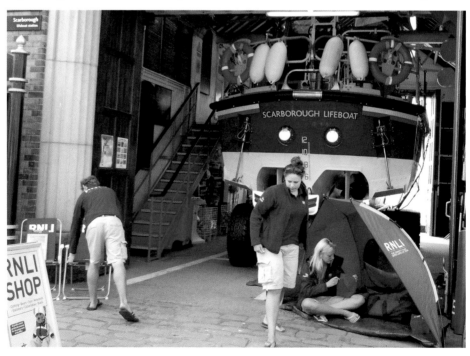

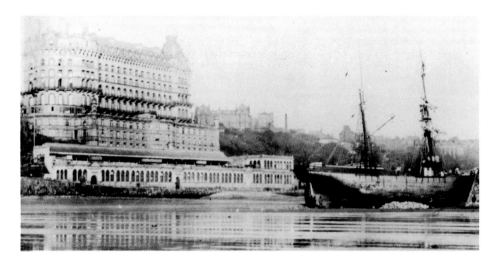

The *Glastry*

The schooner *Glastry* was one of the many ships in trouble off Scarborough during the great storm of 27 October to 30 October 1880; the lifeboat on service was the *Lady Leigh*. The *Scarborough Mercury* reported: 'As soon as daylight appeared, crowds of people thronged the cliffs, gasping with anxious eyes across the wild expanse of water, which for miles around was foaming and seething with terrible fury.' Before ending up on the beach the *Glastry* collided with the brig *Lily*. Other vessels in distress were the *Mary*, the *Jeune Adolphi* and the *Black Eyed Susan*. The crew of the *Glastry* left the ship before it broke free and drifted off again. The modern picture shows a 1914 Vickers Pattern 13-pounder gun raised 100 feet from the seabed by Scarborough Sub Aqua Club and local fishermen in 1982. It was originally on the SS *Hornsund* – a British cargo ship – which was sunk by a German torpedo in 1917, two and a half miles off Scarborough.

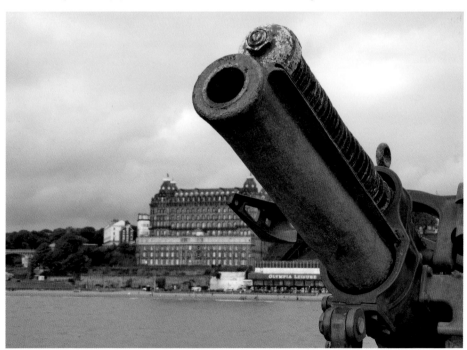

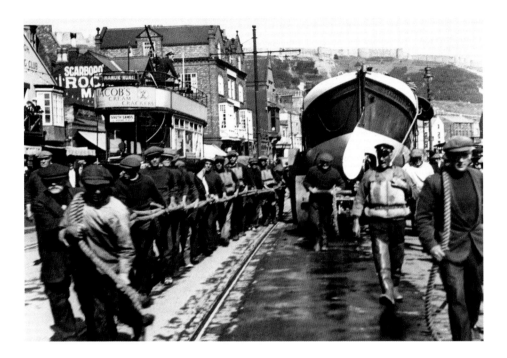

The *Herbert Joy*

The *Herbert Joy* was a self-righting motor lifeboat stationed at Scarborough between 1924 and 1931. The *Herbert Joy II* succeeded her and was, in turn, succeeded by the *ECJR* from 1951–'56. The most remembered rescue by the *ECJR* was probably in December 1951 when she went to the assistance of the Dutch coaster, the *Westkust*. Ten of the crew were saved from the sinking ship, but tragically the last man off was crushed between the two vessels and died on the way back to port. Three years later the *ECJR* capsized in the entrance to the harbour with the loss of three crewmen. The new picture shows the old boathouse from 1914, now part of an amusement arcade.

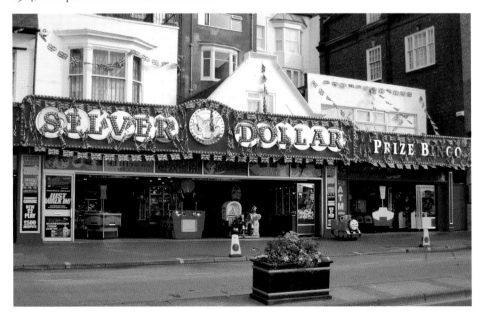

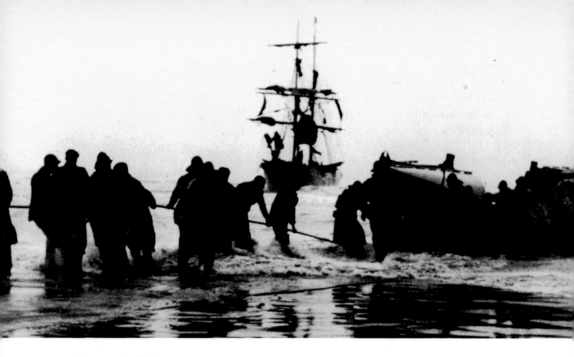

The Wreck of the *Boxer*

13 November 1901 saw a storm raging off Scarborough. The *Edward & Lucille* (1900–'02) went to the aid of the stricken brigantine *Boxer en route* to Hartlepool with a cargo of chalk; beached in South Bay its eight man crew were successfully taken off and the wreck was sold for £8. Scarborough's lifeboat station, established in 1801, is the third oldest in the United Kingdom after Sunderland and Montrose. Thomas Hinderwell, the Scarborough historian, was the impetus for the establishment of a lifeboat here. In 1799 he told of an heroic rescue involving four Scarborough fishermen who rowed in an open coble from Scarborough to a ship in distress off Filey, and of other acts of bravery in other rescues. This led to his campaign for a lifeboat in 1800.

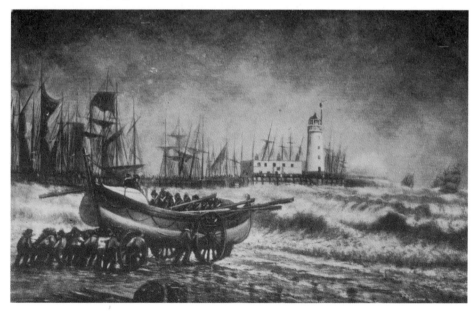

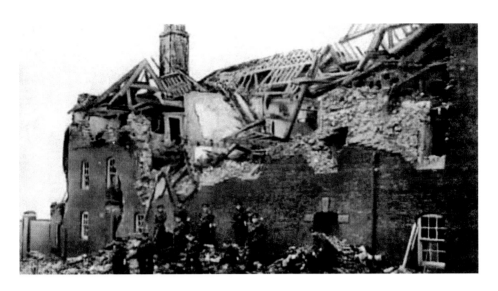

Coastguard Station Shelled, 1914

Scarborough was to be one of four north-east coastal towns bombarded by the German fleet on the morning of 16 December 1914. In the space of forty minutes about 1,000 shells were unleashed on Hartlepool and West Hartlepool from three German heavy cruisers *Blucher*, *Seydlitz* and *Moltke*, killing 63 civilians and 9 soldiers in Hartlepool and 56 civilians in West Hartlepool; 400 or so civilians were injured and much housing stock was damaged or destroyed. The raid on Hartlepool was followed by similar assaults on Scarborough and Whitby, in which eighteen and three people were killed respectively. Off Scarborough the *Derfllinger* and *von der Tann* opened fire on the coastguard station and the barracks before shelling the castle and the Grand Hotel, believing it to be a gun battery. As they passed Whitby they fired fifty rounds at the signal station, town and abbey. The attack on the east coast caused outrage in Britain – partly because the Royal Navy failed to intercept the Germans, but also because Whitby and Scarborough, unlike Hartlepool, were undefended, open towns. The German Navy was not the only destructive force at play in Scarborough as this postcard of the storm damage on the Spa wall by Harry Wanless clearly shows.

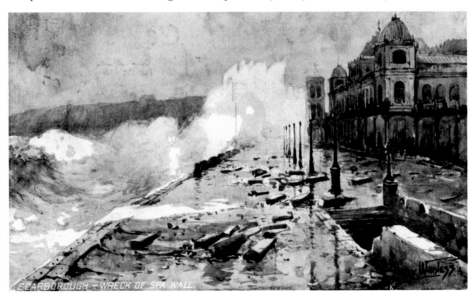

SCARBOROUGH - WRECK OF SPA WALL.

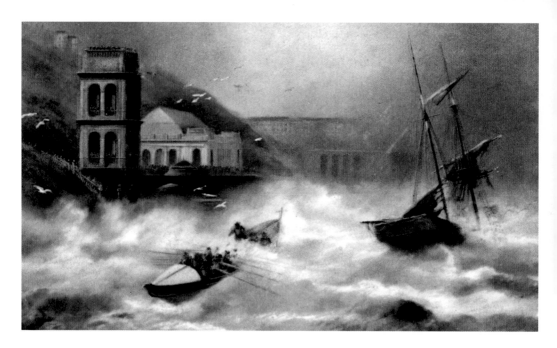

Wreck of the Coupland, 2 November 1861

An 1861 painting by Elmer Keene. The *Coupland*, a South Shields schooner, was in difficulty trying to enter Scarborough harbour. The *Amelia* was called out only to find herself in trouble; her coxswain was swept overboard as the boat was dashed against the sea wall. Three men on the beach, including Lord Charles Beauclerc, died assisting in the rescue; two lifeboat men also died. The cox was saved, but was 'much injured and has been confined to his room ever since'. Twenty-four men died that day in various incidents along the coast; the six men on the *Coupland* were saved and looked after in the Dolphin Inn. The modern photograph shows calmer days off Scarborough harbour.

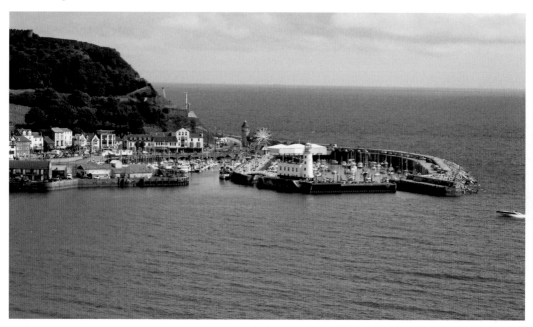

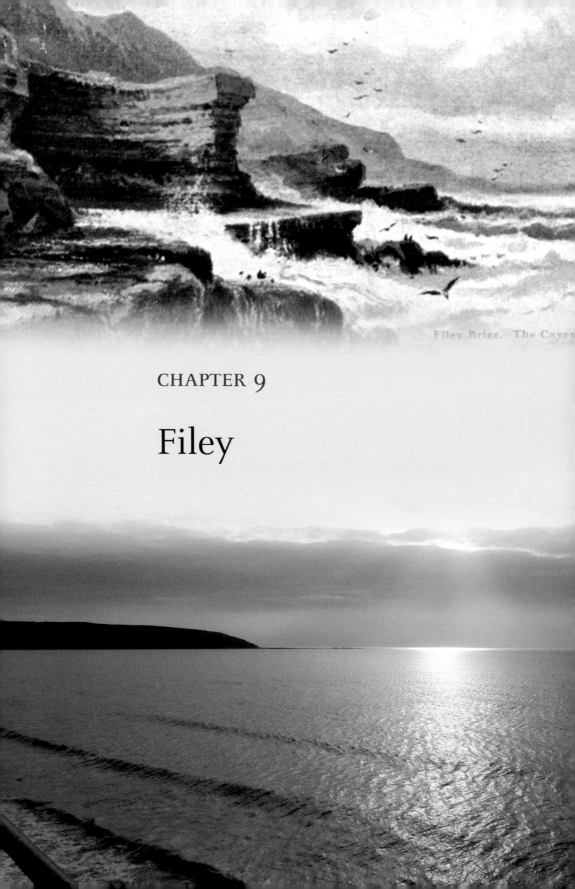

Filey Brigg. - The Caves

CHAPTER 9

Filey

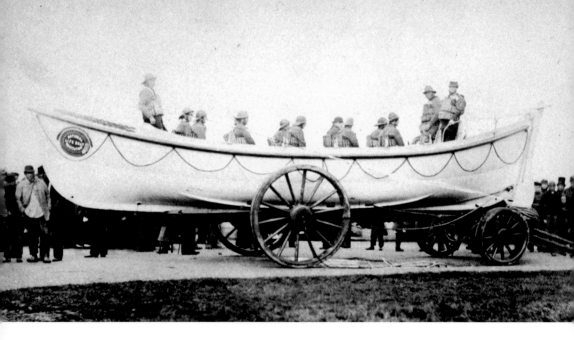

Hollon II, 1863, and the *Keep Fit Association*

Hollon II served Filey between 1884 and 1907. The station at Filey was founded in 1804 and in 1824 Filey residents collected enough money to pay for their own lifeboat, which was built by Skelton of Scarborough. In 1890 a new boathouse was built. The modern photograph shows the *Keep Fit Association*, the current lifeboat. One of the services in 2012 involved the evacuation of four people at a flooded caravan park in Cayton Bay.

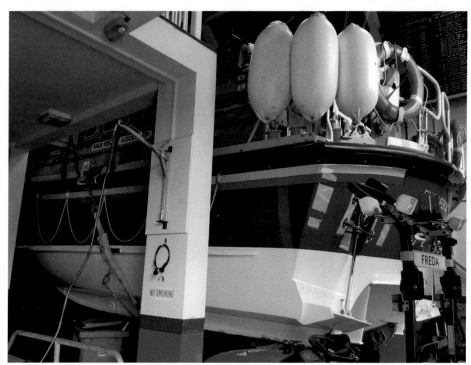

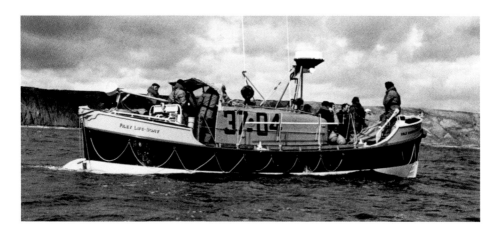

Isa & Penryn Milsted

The *Isa & Penryn Milsted* was stationed at Filey between 1953 and 1968. The *Scarborough Mercury* of 2 June 1860 reported a hurricane that hit Filey. It came 'so suddenly upon the coast that, in ten minutes, the calmness of the bay and neighbouring waters was changed to a boiling flood'. Boats and nets belonging to the local fisherman were all destroyed. On 9 June the *Scarborough Mercury* published a letter sent by a Dr Cortis of Filey to the editor of the *Times*. It read, 'Sir, The *Times* frequently chronicles shipwrecks which occur in this bay, and almost as often has to add, "The crew were saved by the Filey Lifeboat". A short time since it was stated at one of the meetings of the National Institute that this boat had saved more lives than any other in England, and during my own residence here, of nearly twenty years, I know that in every shipwreck our fishermen have cheerfully pushed to the rescue – men having often to be called out of the boat from too many volunteering, but never to be urged into it – and, after saving the lives of the crews, have taken them to their homes and supplied them with warm clothing and other necessities ... Many of these men who have so often helped others are themselves now urgently requiring assistance. The gale of Monday last has not only destroyed their property, but has also deprived them of the means of a livelihood.' He concludes by saying that the men were deserving of help since 'a more industrious, sober, well disposed set of men cannot be found if you search the Kingdom through'. The newer image depicts the *Robert & Dorothy Hardcastle*.

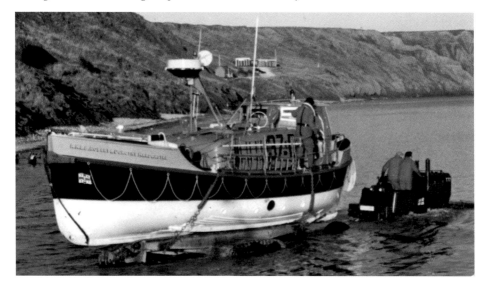

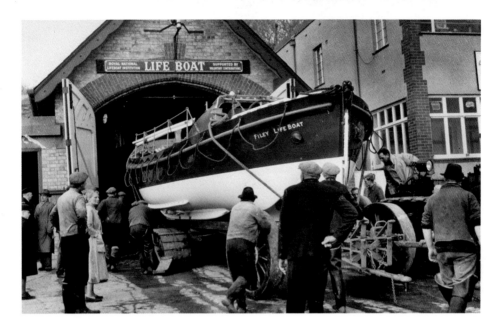

Charles Dickens & Filey

Charles Dickens visited Filey and recorded these observations in his *Household Words* in 1851: 'The sea-side churchyard is a strange witness of the perilous life of the mariner and the fisherman. It is only by a walk in it that we acquire a clear conception of the real nature of that mode of livelihood which such hundreds of thousands, all round these islands, embrace, as a choice or a necessity ... Filey, a mere village, well known to thousands of summer tourists for the noble extent of its sands, and the stern magnificence of its so-called bridge, or promontory of savage rocks running far into the sea, on which you may walk, at low-water; but which, with the advancing tide, becomes savagely grand, from the fury with which the ocean breaks over it. In tempestuous weather this bridge is truly a bridge of sighs to mariners, and many a noble ship has been dashed to pieces upon it. One of the first headstones which catches your eye in the little quiet churchyard of Filey bears witness to the terrors of the bridge. "In memory of Richard Richardson, who was unfortunately drowned December 27, 1799, aged forty-eight years" ...'

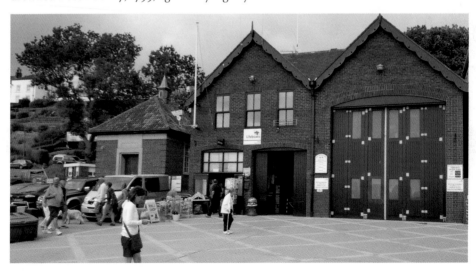

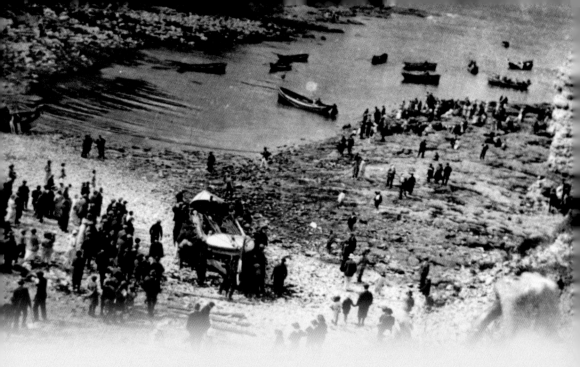

CHAPTER 10

Flamborough

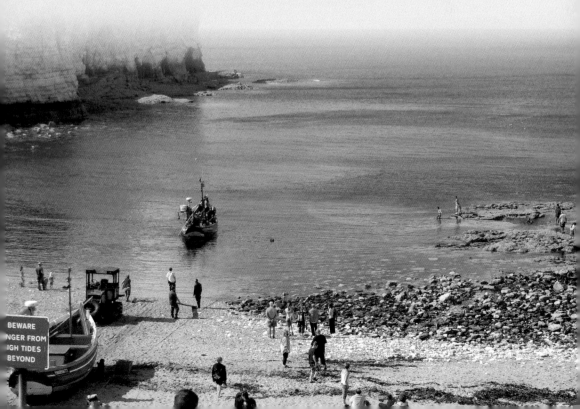

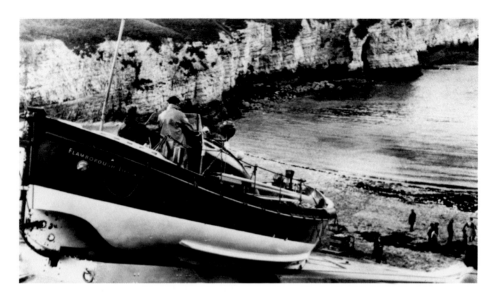

Launching the Flamborough Lifeboat

Flamborough was for many years a shipwreck waiting to happen. The headland juts out into the North Sea by 6 miles, its cliffs are 400 feet high, the scars below are many and razor sharp, and the currents treacherous. Indeed, between 1770 and 1806, 174 ships were wrecked here leading to the construction of a lighthouse in 1806. The 92-foot-high lighthouse pictured on page 66 was brick built from the inside without the use of any scaffolding. It is still in operation today with a light equivalent to three and half million candle power visible up to 21 miles away. On 10 February 1871 a violent storm hit Bridlington Bay with the loss of over seventy seamen and thirty ships. It was after this disaster that the lifeboat stations at Flamborough were established. Two lifeboat stations were built – one at North Landing, and the other at South Landing, pictured here. The idea was to ensure that that at least one of the lifeboats could be launched into the lee of a gale. The local fishermen had been doing this for years, keeping cobles at both landings.

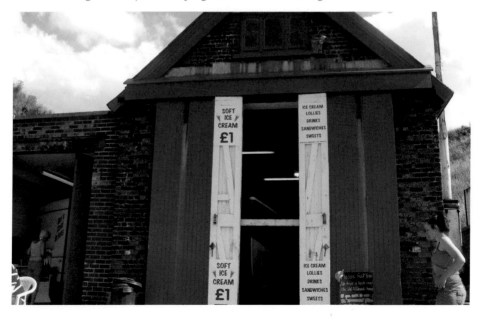

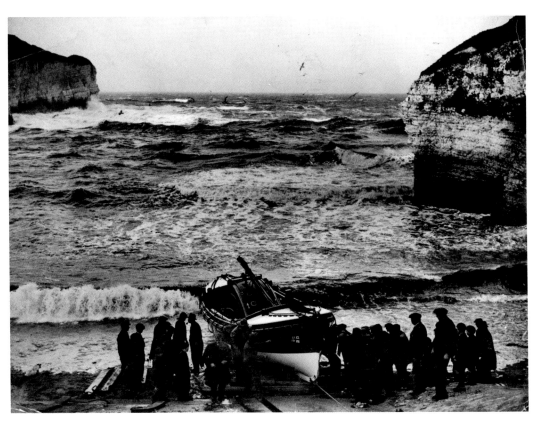

The *Friendly Forester* 1953–1983

The £15,738 cost of the lifeboat was met by the Ancient Order of Foresters Friendly Society who requested the boat be named thus and that the bow and arrow emblem feature on her bows.

The bow is the bow of benevolence and the arrow signifies speedy assistance. The equipment carried on board included: an echo sounder for recording the depth of water under the keel; a Schermuly rocket line; breeches buoy; a Redifon ultra-high frequency (UHF) radio telephone and a Coastal Curlew MF radio telephone to communicate with other vessels and the coastguard; an Aldis signalling lamp for use in the event of radio communications failing; an electric searchlight and fifteen white parachute flares; and self-heating tins of soup and cocoa. The South Landing station was demolished in 1992 and re-built to house the new Atlantic lifeboat. It had been closed in 1938 and became a fisherman's store. The original North Landing station still survives as a café and small museum. The *Friendly Forester* was replaced by the Oakley design *Will & Fanny Kirby*, which saw service until 1993. The chalk tower was built in 1674 and is the oldest surviving complete lighthouse in England.

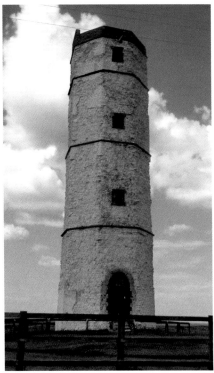

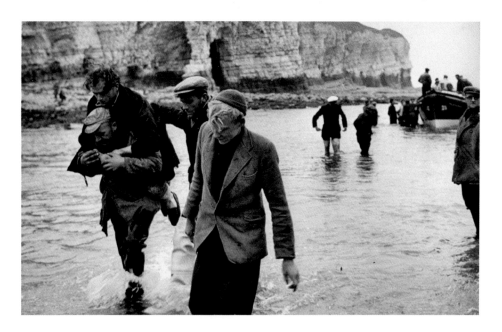

How Does a Self-righting Lifeboat Work?

The *Will & Fanny Kirby* was a self-righting lifeboat. How this works is lucidly explained by Simon Robson on his *Flamborough Lifeboats* website, at www.sprobson.f2s.com – 'the Oakley design was the first to combine inherent stability with the ability to self-right in the event of capsizing. The righting was achieved by system of shifting water ballast. On launching, the lifeboat took on 1½ tons of sea water into a tank in the bottom of the hull. If the lifeboat reached a crucial point of capsize the water transferred, through valves to a righting tank on the port side. If the capsize was to the starboard side, the water transfer started when an angle of 165° was reached. This would push the boat into completing a full 360° roll. If the capsize was to the port side, the water transfer started at 110°. This weight of water combined with the weight of machinery usually managed to stop the roll and allow the lifeboat to "bounce back".' The current lifeboat, since 2007, is the *Elizabeth Jane Palmer*.

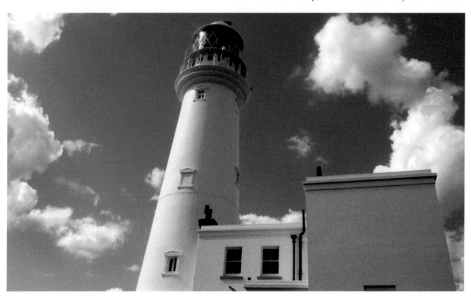

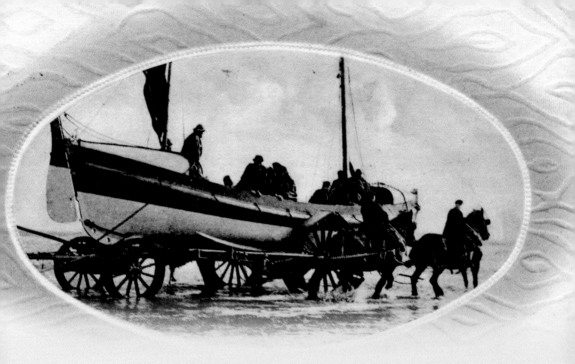

CHAPTER 11

Bridlington

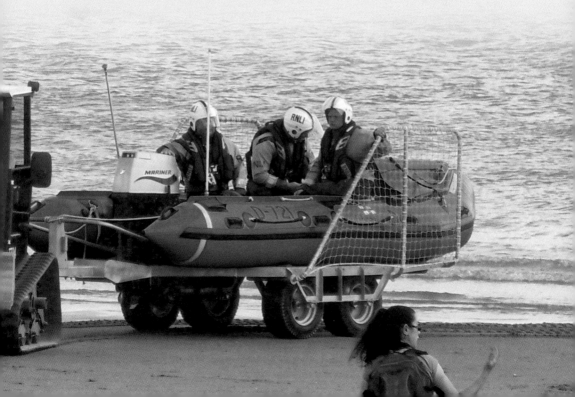

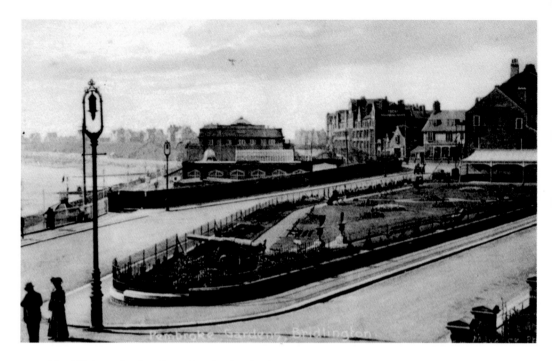

The Lifeboat Station from Pembroke Gardens

Note the cannon in the foreground 'guarding' the town since 1910. The first lifeboat, a Greathead, came in 1806. In 1824 this was replaced by one of the lifeboats donated by the Royal National Institute for the Preservation of Life from Shipwreck and served Bridlington until 1865. The new photograph shows the *Marine Engineer* on Lifeboat Day in 2012; the inshore lifeboat *Windsor Spirit* is on pages 67 and 72.

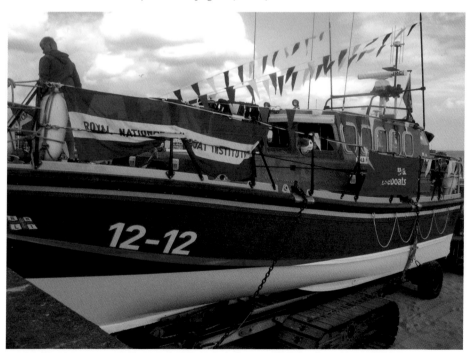

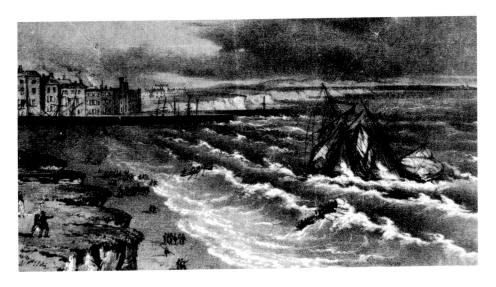

The Wreck of the *Omega*

On 27 December 1852, after some delay when the lifeboat committee refused to launch the lifeboat because this required the approval of two committee members, the lifeboat was finally launched, but none of the three crew members on the *Omega* were saved. A new committee was formed to ensure that such mindless officiousness never stood in the way of a rescue again. Such was the terrible reputation of the seas around Bridlington and Flamborough that Bridlington Bay was known as the bay of safety. To give an idea of the maritime activity in the area at the end of the eighteenth century there was frequently up to 300 boats moored in Bridlington Bay at any one time. Between 1770 and 1806, 174 ships came to grief off the town. The lower picture shows an RAF helicopter winching off the RAF air sea rescue launch during a training exercise.

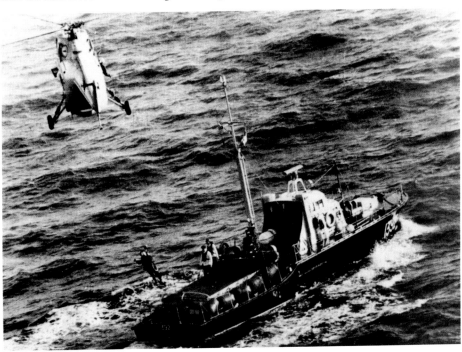

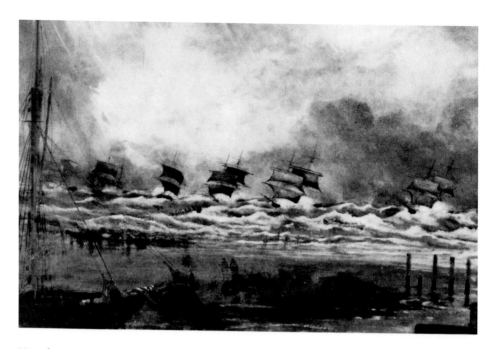

Wreckage on North Beach after the Great Gale, 1871

The pictures show collier brigantines driven ashore during the storm and the aftermath. Both Bridlington's lifeboats – the private *Harbinger* and the RNLI *Robert Whitworth* – fought valiantly to help the stricken boats. The *Robert Whitworth* went out three times and saved sixteen lives before it was withdrawn from the service; the *Harbinger* went out eight times before it capsized with the loss of six lives, trying to save the *Delta*. Thirty ships and seventy lives were lost that night in and around the bay of safety.

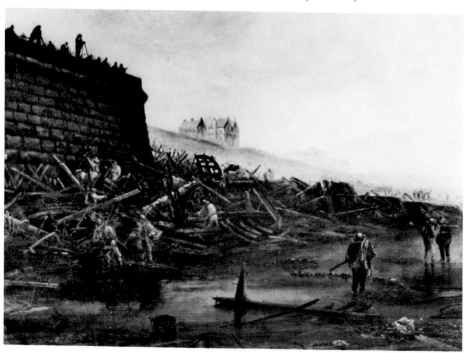

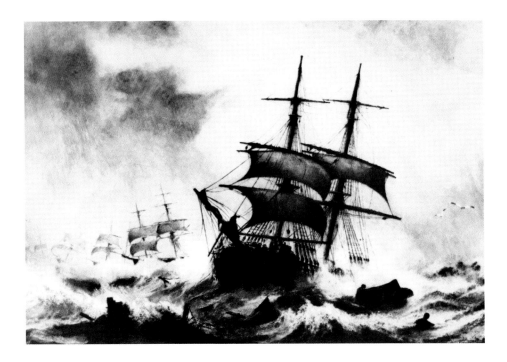

The *Stanhope Smart,* 1931–1947

The lower picture shows the *Stanhope Smart* in January 1934 when one of the crew was swept overboard but later recovered and hauled back on board. The first *Robert Whitworth* was unpopular with the crew. This resulted in a Hungarian nobleman, Count Batthyány, commissioning a local joiner, David Purdon, to build a lifeboat to the fishermen's specifications, and so was born the *Harbinger*. Later, the RNLI commissioned a new *Robert Whitworth*, again to the specifications of the fishermen, and this replaced the original *Robert Whitworth*. The other photograph is the *Harbinger* capsizing in the Great Gale of 1871.

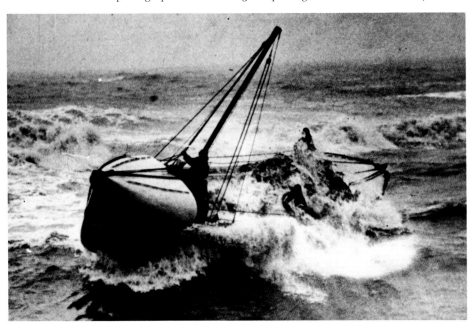

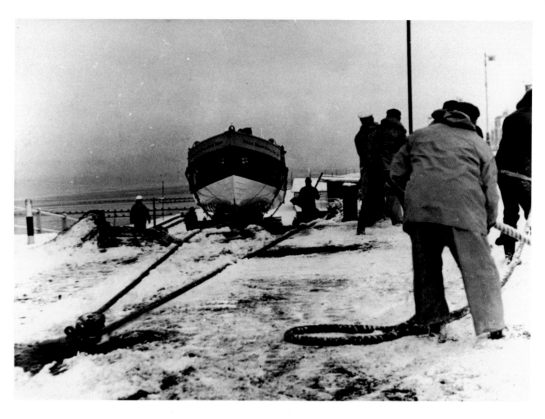

William, Henry & Mary King

The *Stanhope Smart* took over in August 1931 – Bridlington's first motor lifeboat. She was launched sixty times, saved fifty-three lives and served until 1947. The *William, Henry & Mary King* arrived in 1967; she launched 290 times and saved 83 lives between 1967 and 1988.

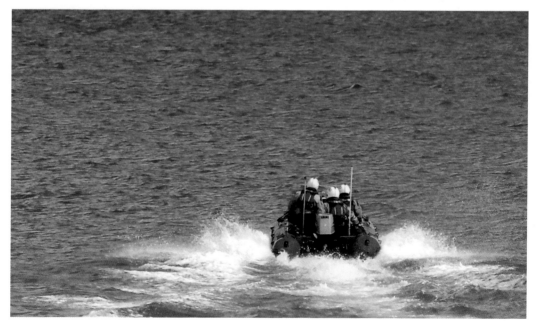

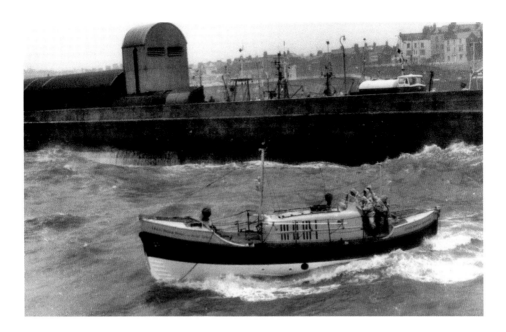

The Bridlington Lifeboat Houses

The current lifeboat house was built in 1903. In 1806 the first lifeboat house was at the end of Chapel Street. In 1865 a new lifeboat house was built opposite the end of what is now Windsor Crescent. The boat was launched by towing it on a carriage down the slipway at the end of the South Pier, or at Trinity Cut on the north side, by horses through the town. A second lifeboat, built in 1866, was kept at the harbour and operated by the fishermen. The pictures show the *William, Henry & Mary King* and a busy Bridlington harbour today.

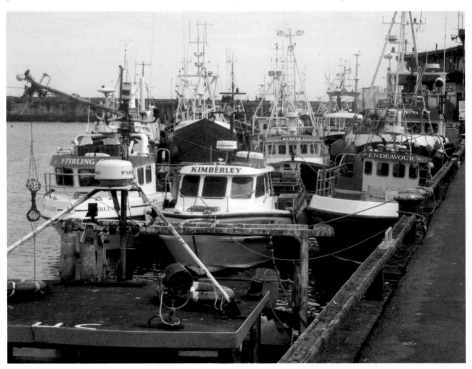

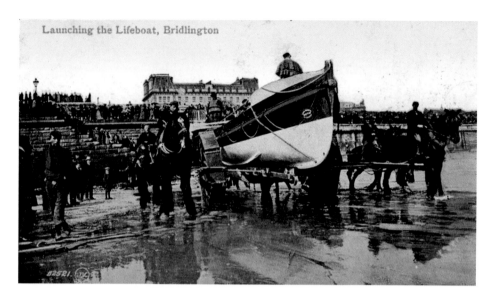

Launching the Lifeboat, Bridlington

George & Jane Walker and Lawrence of Arabia

The top picture shows the *William John & Frances* being launched in the 1880s. From the 1920s, 21 Air Sea Rescue Unit operated from where the Lawrence building is now until 1978. In 1932 T. E. Shaw, or Lawrence of Arabia, stayed here to train the crews of the armoured target boats of RAF 1104 Marine Craft Unit. He stayed at the Bay View Hotel, reputedly sleeping with a dagger on a chair next to the bed. On later visits in 1933, 1934 and 1935, he stayed in the tower room at the Ozone Hotel, now the Royal Yorkshire yacht club.

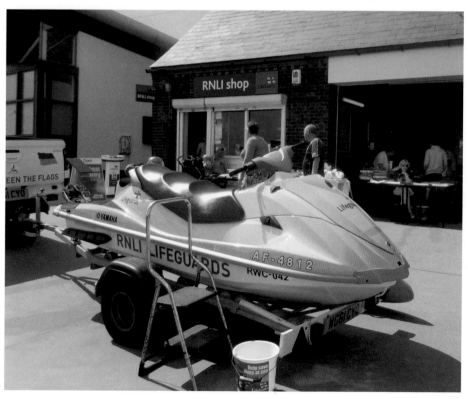

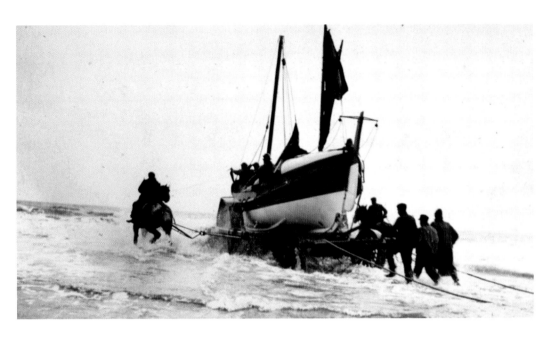

Launching the *George & Jane Walker* with Horses

Bridlington has two lifeboat houses. The all weather lifeboat house is on South Marine Drive opposite the Spa Royal Hall, to the south of the harbour. The inshore lifeboat house is on Princess Mary Promenade. During the First World War on 18 March 1915 the *George & Jane Walker* was called out to rescue a sinking minesweeper in atrocious weather. During the launch two horses were entangled in the lifeboat carriage and subsequently drowned, along with Robert Carr, one of the riders. Sadly the twelve sailors on the minesweeper also perished.

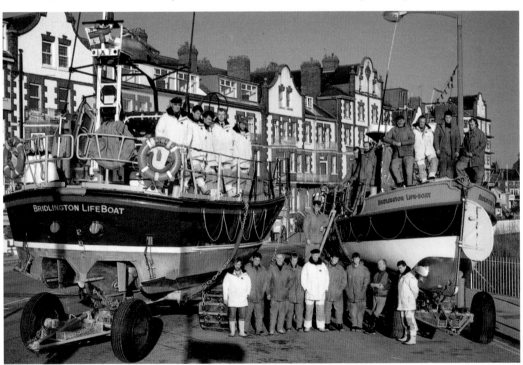

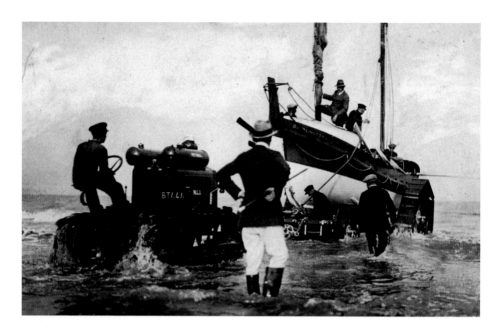

Launching the *George & Jane Walker* with a Caterpillar Tractor

A tractor launch around 1921. There were two lifeboats bearing that name here. The first was a temporary replacement for the damaged *William John & Frances* for one year in 1898. The second arrived in 1899 with fifty-eight launches and fifty lives saved up to 1931. The *Marine Engineer* on Lifeboat Day in 2012 is in the new photograph. RNLI lifeguards patrol (*see page 74*) nearly 200 beaches around the UK; in 2011 they saved eighty-four lives and helped 17,671 people to safety.

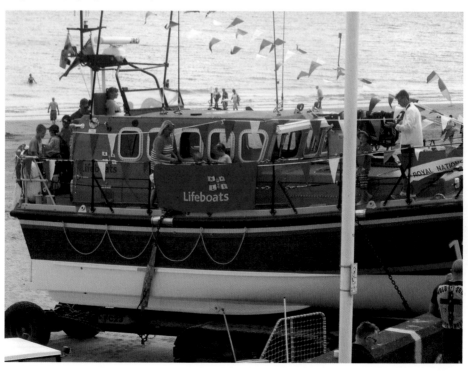

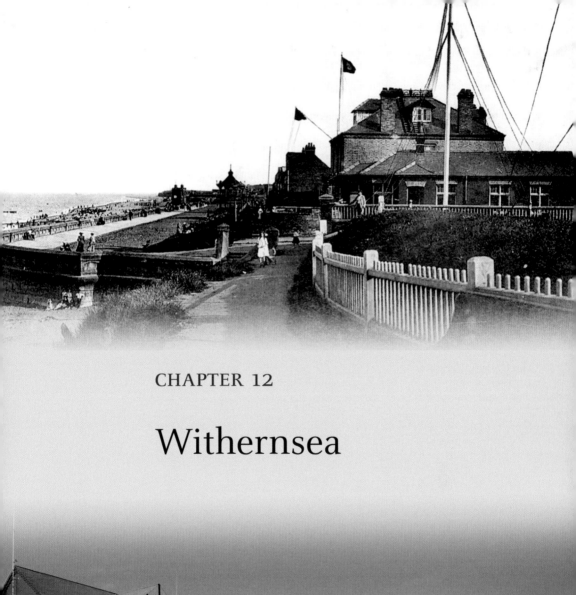

CHAPTER 12

Withernsea

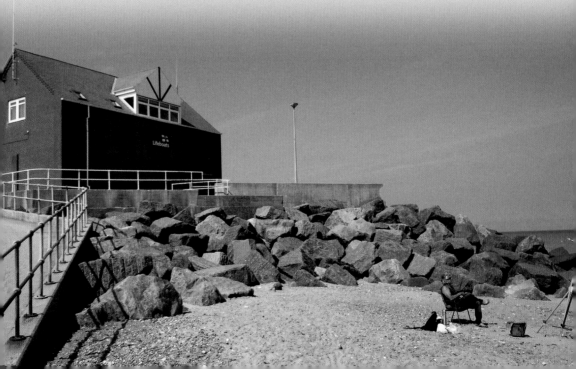

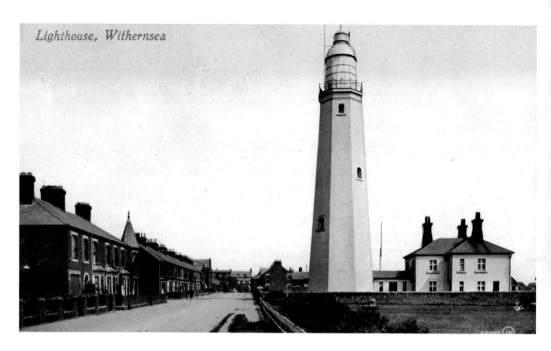

Lighthouse, Withernsea

The Octagonal Lighthouse

In the sixteenth century the coastline around Withernsea was guarded by three beacons; in 1893 these were replaced by the octagonal lighthouse in Arthur Street, shown here in 1913 and in 2012. It is brick and concrete built, and is 120 feet high with 144 steps. The light was first switched on in 1894 and switched off for the last time in 1974. It owes its existence to the coroner at the inquest of the *Genista* disaster in 1890; he concluded that lives might have been saved if the town had had a lighthouse. It now houses a superb lighthouse and lifeboat museum.

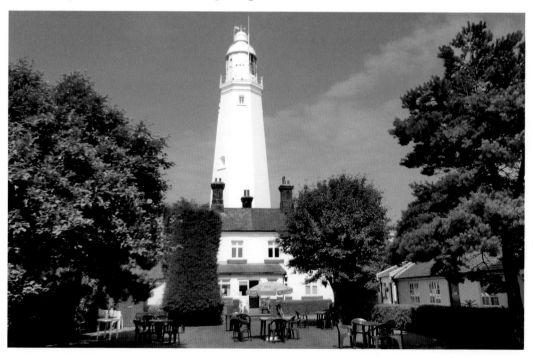

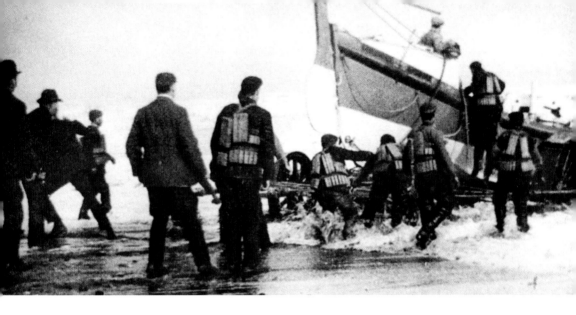

The *Admiral Rous*

Boarding the *Admiral Rous*, during a launch, and a similar operation in 2011 on the *Henley Eight*. The *Admiral Rous* was one of two lifeboats – the other was *Admiral Rous II* – bequeathed by Admiral Rous along with a boathouse in 1877 and 1882 respectively. The first lifeboat station here was built in 1862 with a boathouse in Arthur Street. Rous' boathouse in Seaside Road replaced it in 1882 and was in use until 1913. The Arthur Street building became the rocket store. The coastguard station on Marine Parade (*see page 81*) was built in 1905 and was in service until 1951. The lifeboat station also closed in 1913 and the boat moved to Easington when a motor-powered boat started operations from the Humber station. It was, nevertheless, reopened in 1974.

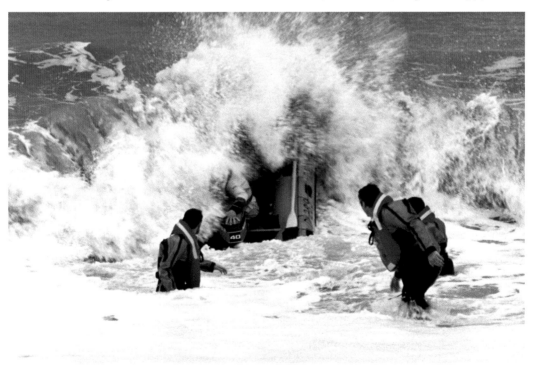

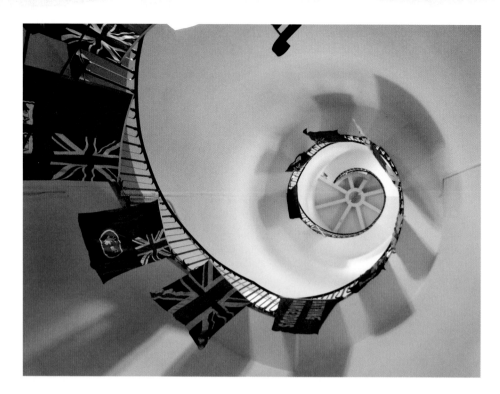

The Kegworth Plane Crash

There were additional lifeboat stations to the north at Hornsea from 1852 to 1924, and at Barmston from 1884 to 1898. To the south, the *Docea Chapman* served Easington from 1913 to 1933. Perhaps the most dramatic service undertaken by the Withernsea crew was during the January 1989 Kegworth M1 Boeing 737 crash where they assisted for 3 hours recovering 126 dead and many more injured; the crew were in a minibus coming home from the London Boat Show. The pictures show the inside of the lighthouse looking to the top with some of the many steps, and a launch of the lifeboat at Withernsea.

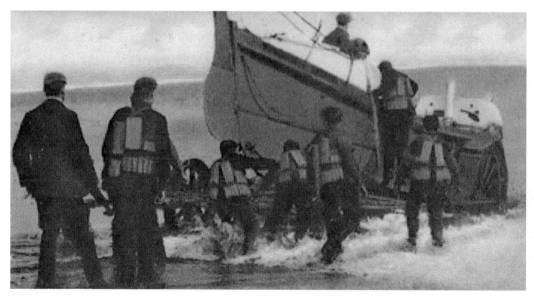

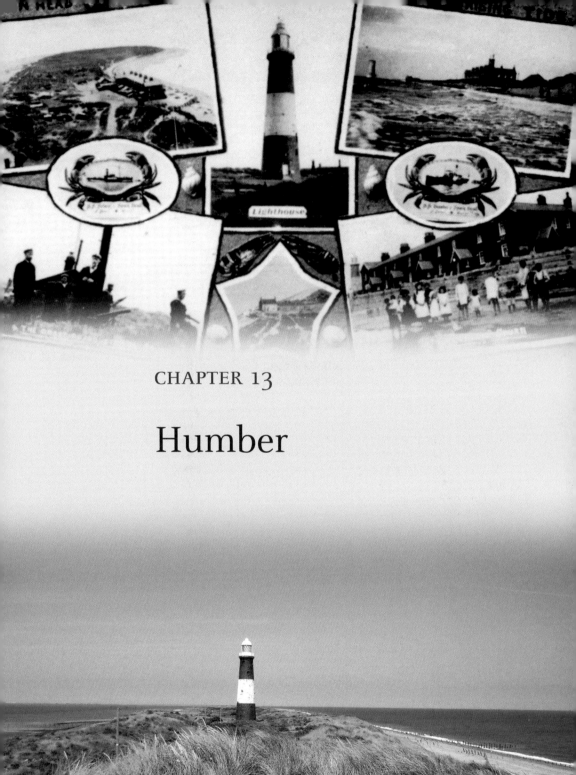

CHAPTER 13

Humber

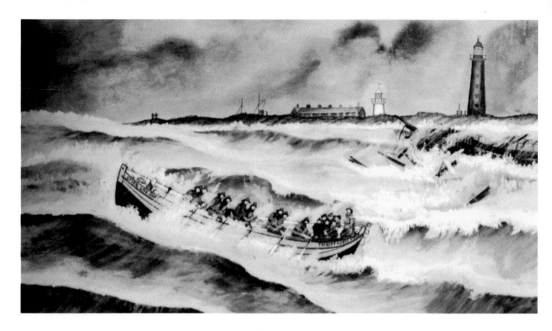

The Trinity House Lifeboats

The 1892 *Bulmer's Directory of the East Riding* called Spurn Point 'a wild and dreary spot'. Dreary it certainly is not, with its beautiful wilderness; wild it certainly can be, as the history of the lifeboat station here so eloquently proves. The crew of the Trinity House boat depicted here in an 1850s painting would certainly agree. A new Trinity boat arrived in 1852. The Humber lifeboat is unique in that, due to the remoteness of their station, it is the only station fully manned by employees of the RNLI; all other crews, of course, are volunteers. The contemporary photograph shows the *Pride of the Humber* today moored at the end of the pier.

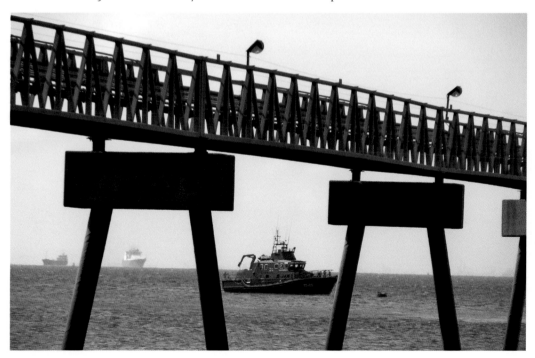

Spurn Lifeboat Men, c. 1890

The Trinity House boat, according to Hull Trinity House, had saved 729 lives between 1810 and 1850. The men here are wearing the usual cork lifejackets or life-preservers as they were then known, which had been issued by Hull from 1841. They are on their lifeboat built in 1881. The first lifeboat station opened in 1810 when Trinity House in Hull provided a Greathead lifeboat after a Mr Iverson offered to recruit a twelve-man crew, convert the barracks on Spurn into cottages and a tavern, thus providing a living for the master. A new boathouse was built in 1854. A detail from the mural painted by Les Porter forms the new picture; for more of his work see www.lesporterartist.co.uk.

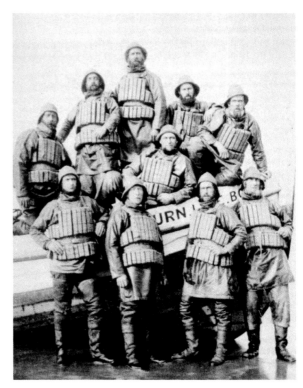

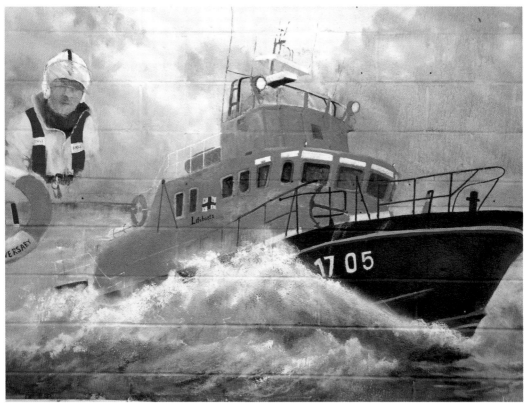

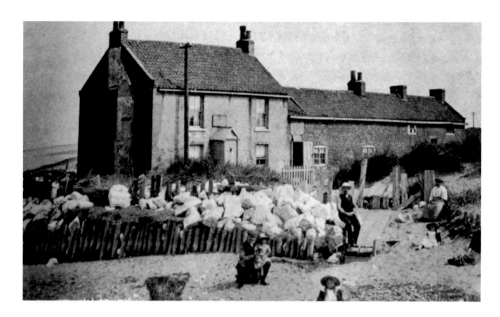

The Second Lifeboat Inn

This is the second Lifeboat Inn at Spurn, built largely from the bricks from the demolished lifeboat cottages around 1860. Mr James Hopper, the innkeeper, can be seen in the foreground along with his family. The chalk was dumped here to protect the inn. The first Lifeboat Inn, or Tavern, or, according to the OS map, the Lifeboat Hotel, was a converted barracks and home to the master of the Spurn lifeboat station. Apart from selling drink and provisions the master, in common with his fellow crew members, made money from loading gravel from the beaches onto ships. The new cottages, built in 1819, were superseded in 1858 by a row of cottages, which were inhabited until 1975. The new photograph shows the lifeboat families' houses today; however, the six families who live here moved out in August 2012 due to the difficulties of living on the peninsula with its increasing erosion. Their homes are being converted into dormitories and offices. The lifeboat will still have a full crew; four new members have been recruited to work the shift system where five members work six days on and six days off.

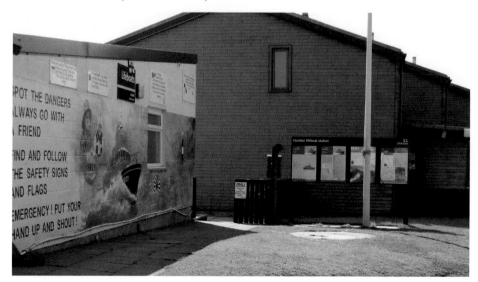

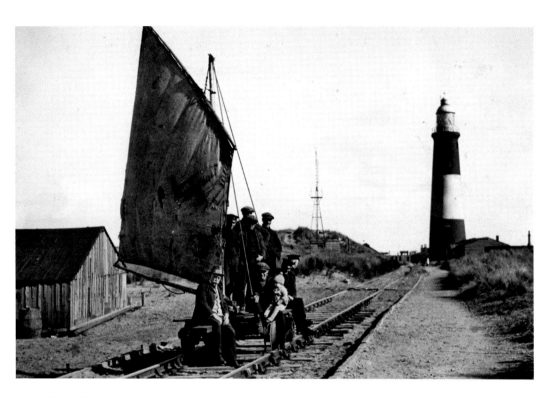

The Sail-powered Bogie

This was used as transport along the peninsula until the 1930s. The lifeboat men shared the line with the railways; it was used by the Army during the Second World War and was closed in 1951. Compare the similar photograph in the Redcar chapter on page 35. A third Trinity lifeboat took over in 1881. On a stormy night in 1883, however, when the lifeboat men prepared to return to their boat after an all night on watch, they found that it had gone. It was later discovered drifting off the island of Texel, off the north coast of the Netherlands. Her boarding boat suffered a similar fate in 1888 when it was washed away and ended up, damaged beyond repair, at Great Yarmouth.

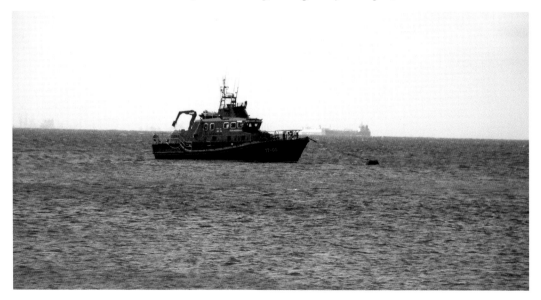

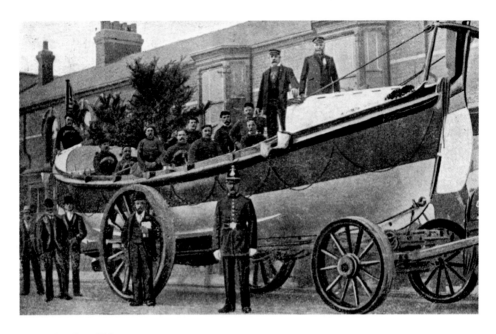

The Grimsby Lifeboat Crew, 1904

Two pictures of the RNLI's *Manchester Unity*, which was loaned to Spurn Point in 1901–02, while a new Trinity lifeboat was being built. The station passed under the control of the Humber Conservancy Board in 1908 and was then taken over by the RNLI in 1911. They replaced the old trinity boat in 1913 with their *Charles Deere James*.

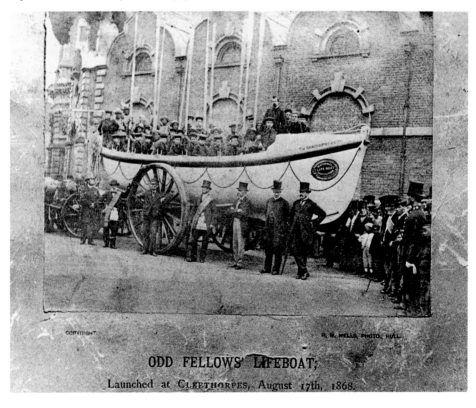

ODD FELLOWS' LIFEBOAT;
Launched at CLEETHORPES, August 17th, 1868.

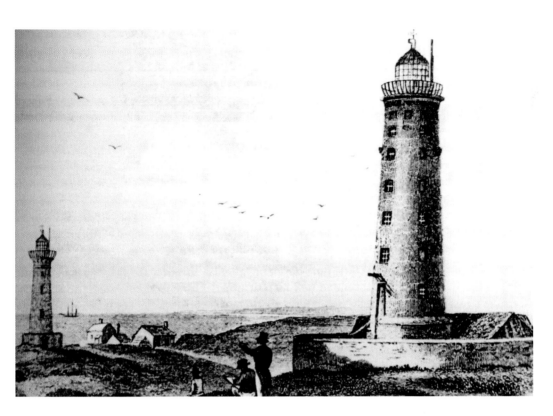

Spurn Head Life

Apart from the lifeboat crew, Spurn was home to the lighthouse keepers and their families, the landlord of the inn and his family, a teacher and staff at the Lloyd's signal station and the coastguards. At its peak the population was over 130. The first lighthouse was built here in 1427, followed by others in a bid to ensure a degree of safety from the ever shifting sandbanks at the mouth of the estuary. The last lighthouse dates from 1895 and saw service until 1986.

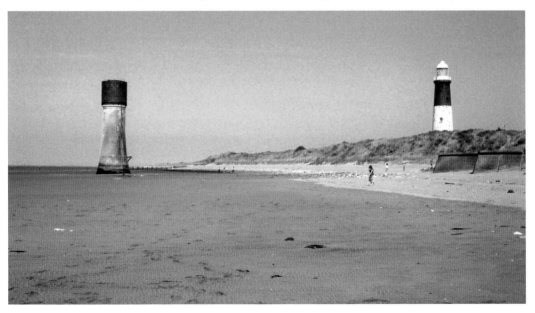

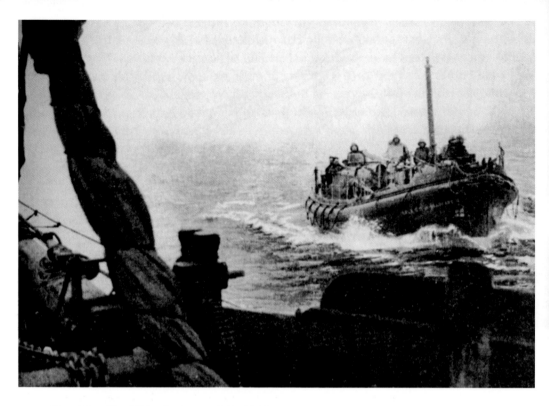

City of Bradford II in the Second World War
The *City of Bradford II* approaching a fishing boat sometime during the Second World War; the machine gun is clearly visible. The *City of Bradford II* started its service in 1929 and was retired in 1954. The newer picture shows the *Kenneth Thelwall*, which came into service in 1987.

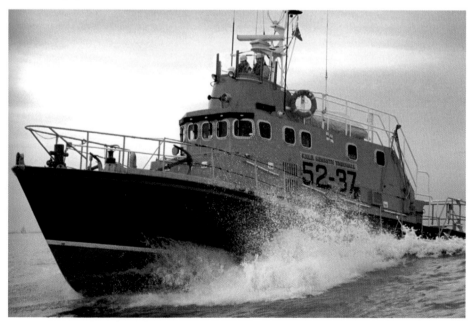

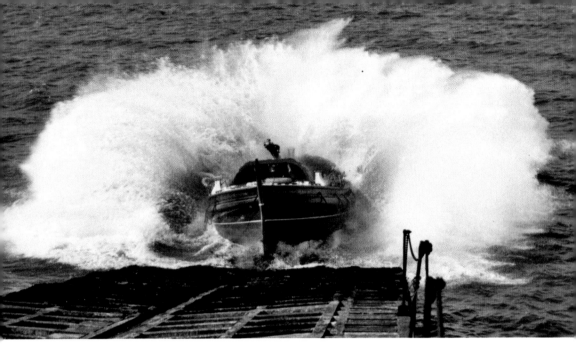

Launch of *City of Bradford II*

Here it is again at one of its launches. Robert Cross, one of the most decorated lifeboat men ever, retired in February 1944 having spent much of his thirty-one years at Spurn as cox on the *City of Bradford II*. During that time he helped to save 244 lives and had been awarded 2 gold, 3 silver and 2 bronze medals for gallantry – all this in addition to the George Medal he received in 1940.

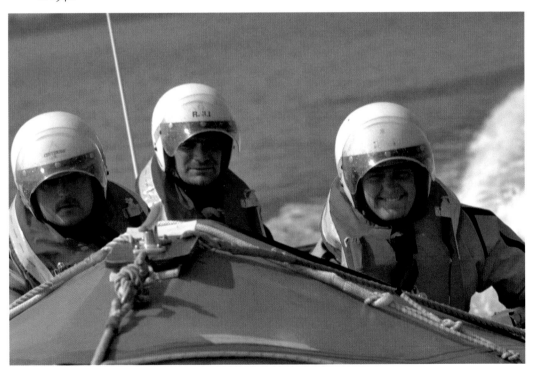

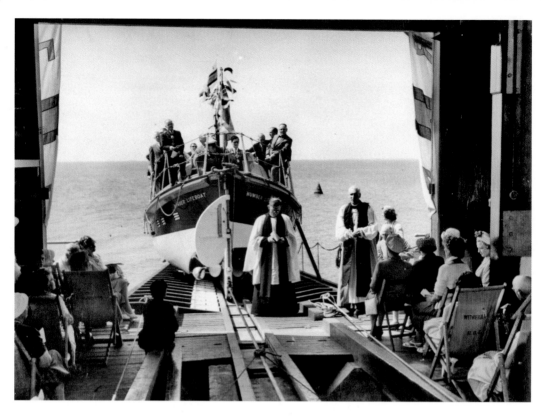

Dedication of *City of Bradford III* **in 1960**
This took place in the boathouse on 22 June 1960 to mark the 150th anniversary of the Humber lifeboat station.

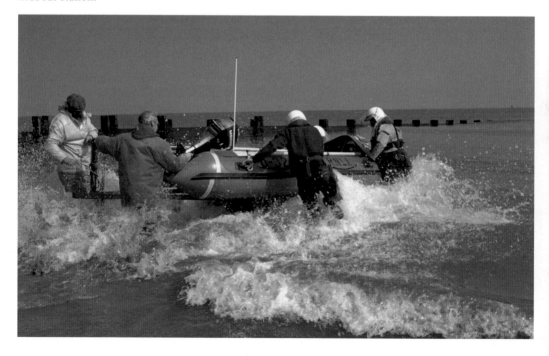

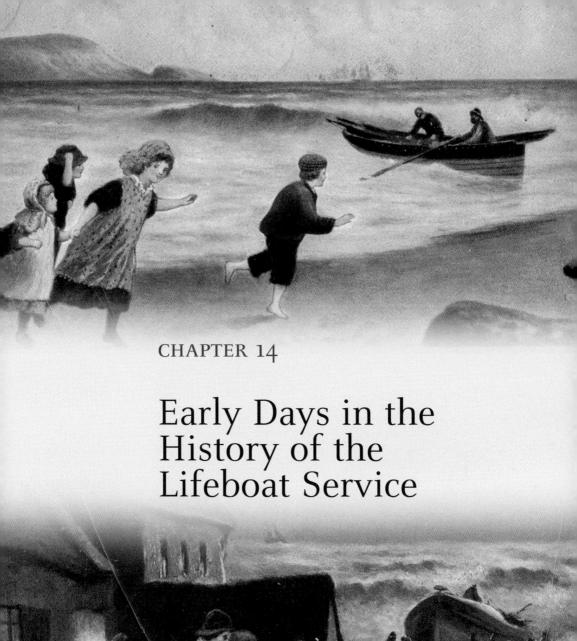

CHAPTER 14

Early Days in the History of the Lifeboat Service

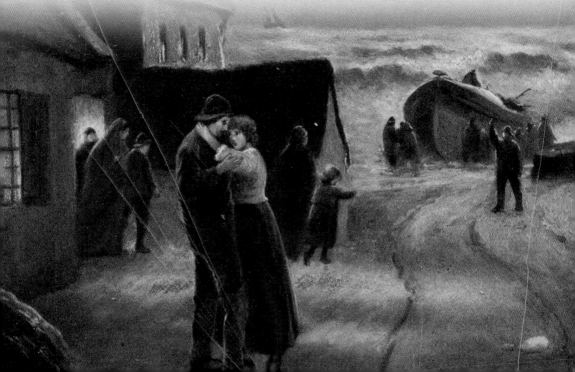

LIFE BELTS FOR LIFE BOATS.

CAPTAIN WARD'S R. N.

(Life Boat Inspector to the Royal National Life Boat Institution.)

CORK WAIST LIFE BELT.

THE ADVANTAGES OF THIS BELT ARE—

1. It secures a large amount of buoyancy, without inconvenience to the wearer, when properly put on.

2. It is perfectly flexible.

3. It affords great protection to the body of the wearer against injury when in the water, and preserves it from cold in severe weather.

4. It is very durable, and not liable to injury, but readily repaired if injured.

5. From being secured tightly round the waist, it cannot slip upwards or downwards when in the water.

☞ These Belts possess buoyant power equal to 24lbs. being double that of ordinary Cork Belts.

RULES TO BE OBSERVED.

Cross the upper corner strings over the opposite shoulders, as braces are worn, and tie them to the short strings in front, pulling the Belt up under the arms. Pass the waist strings round the waist, and tie them tightly together in front.

• This Belt needs to be put on to be appreciated, since though somewhat cumbersome in appearance, it is not felt when on, to be more so than a waistcoat.

To test, however, its full advantages, and its amount of buoyant power, it must be worn in the water.

MANUFACTURED BY

J. BIRT, Jun., Cork Life Belt & Buoy Maker,
5, WELLCLOSE SQUARE, LONDON, E.

N.B.—Tie the Strings as they are when sent, but tighten them to suit the wearer. Those with the striped strings are the larger size, and the green the smaller.

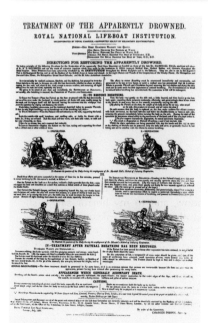

The Ideal Lifeboat Man

On 3 August 1928 the *Scarborough Mercury* published a prize-winning essay entitled 'A Lifeboatman' by Olive Owston, a pupil at Gladstone Road School, Scarborough. 'A lifeboat man should be a total abstainer. This is a very important feature in his character, because he would do more harm than good if he went out in the Lifeboat when he had had a drink. If he took drink he would not be ready for a call at any time; and a lifeboat man should always be ready to go in the lifeboat, even during the middle of a cold, snowy winter night ... work with God, love god, and above all trust god ... a Lifeboat man should always have his ... oilskin and sou'wester in the lifeboat ready for the urgent call. And if there were no time to go home for these things, he could put them on as the boat was being pulled into the sea ... in all spare minutes the lifeboat man should be reading books on the lifeboat, to see if he can learn anything more about his duties on his boat.' The illustrations show an approved lifebelt ('must be worn in water') and the 1852 RNLI *Treatment of the Apparently Drowned.*

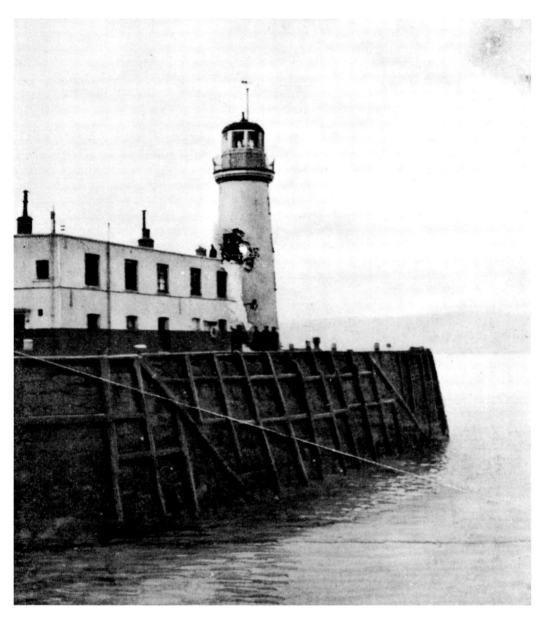

The Scarborough Bombardment

This is how George Rowntree, of the famous confectionery family, in his *Reminiscences*, graphically described the raid: 'I looked through the window, and to my horror saw a shell strike Mr Turner's house, "Dunollie," just below us. Then another terrific explosion, and a mass of smoke and debris rose in the air ... Then came the heaviest firing; the noise was terrific. We could hear the swish, swish of the shells as they came over us and burst on Oliver's Mount. No district in Scarborough escaped. About 300 houses were struck, and the coastguard considered that anywhere up to 500 shells were fired ... Many have left their homes; people fled from the town along the York Road and the trains were filled with rich and poor ... Two ladies left their home on the South Cliff with their long hair down their backs, and in their hurry left their false teeth on the breakfast table. One man put his Christmas cake under his arm and a woman who did not like to leave her best silk dress for the Germans quickly put it on.'

93

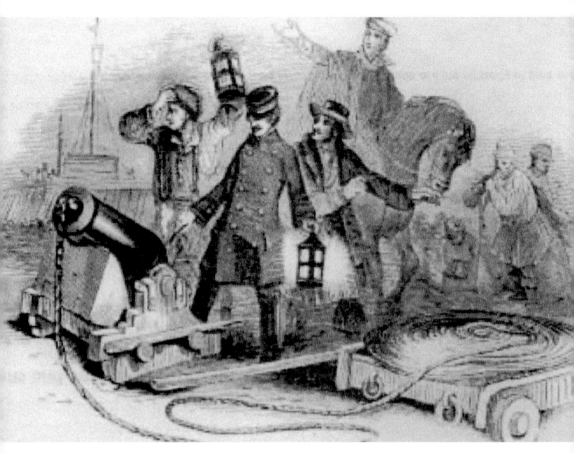

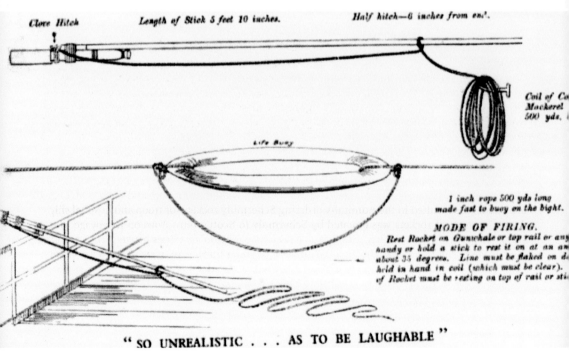

Close Hitch Length of Stick 5 feet 10 inches. Half hitch—6 inches from end.

Coil of Co
Mackerel
500 yds.

Life Buoy

1 inch rope 500 yds long
made fast to buoy on the bight.

MODE OF FIRING.

Rest Rocket on Gunwhale or top rail or any
handy or hold a stick to rest it on at an an
about 35 degrees. Line must be flaked on de
held in hand in coil (which must be clear).
of Rocket must be resting on top of rail or sti

" SO UNREALISTIC . . . AS TO BE LAUGHABLE "

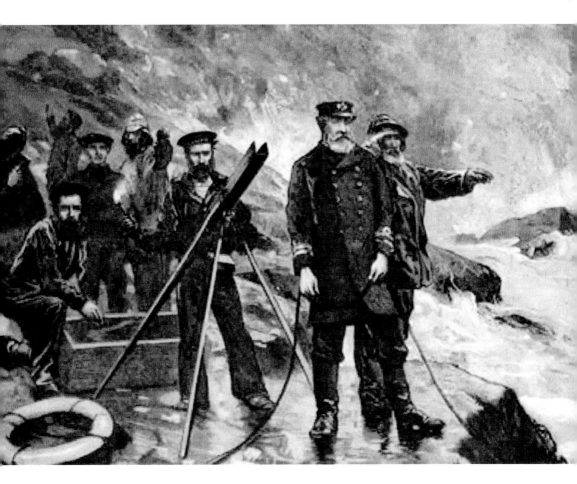

The Volunteer Rocket Brigade

This came into being in the early nineteenth century when Captain George Manby (1765–1854) developed his mortar and rocket-firing rope line equipment to winch sailors marooned on ships close to shore to safety. The first successful deployment was at Great Yarmouth when Manby rescued sailors from the brig *Elizabeth* with his mortar. When an endangered vessel was too far from shore a boat took the rocket brigade out to nearer the ship. At the beginning of the twentieth century William Schermuly (1857–1929) set out to invent a fool-proof rocket system for use in the fiercest of storms. A device already existed – a cannonball with a rope attached (illustrated here) – but this was ineffective and other devices were nothing short of risible. Schermuly's device was efficient and effective although, initially, the Admiralty and ship owners were not interested until, that is, the HMHS *Rohilla* struck a mine off Whitby in 1914 on its way to Belgium to pick up wounded soldiers. Eighty-five crew and many nurses and doctors on board drowned. This resulted in the Admiralty ordering Schermuly rockets for troop and hospital ships. A consignment of rockets was donated by Schermuly to Scott's *Terra Nova* on its voyage to the Antarctic. In 1916 the Canadian Army used them to throw telephone lines between trenches and for sending urgent messages. In 1922 twenty-two shipping lines were using Schermuly rockets; William Schermuly died in 1929, 19 days after it became mandatory for all vessels over 500 tons to carry line throwers under the Merchant Shipping (Line Throwing) Act.

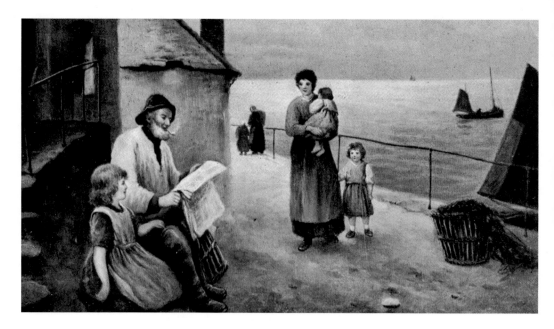

Breeches Buoy

Invented, and originally called *The Bosun's Chair*, by Henry Trengrouse, a cabinet maker born in Helston in 1772. In 1807 he witnessed the sinking of the *Anson* and devoted the rest of his life to inventing life-saving equipment. Initially the government of the day was not interested, but eventually ordered twenty, and started to manufacture Breeches Buoys for themselves, giving Trengrouse a paltry £50. It took a Russian to make amends. Tsar Alexander I gave Trengrouse a diamond ring in recognition of lives saved in the Baltic by the breeches buoy. The illustrations here and on page 91 are from a series of postcards illustrating the lives of lifeboat men and their families. They were published around 1909; these particular ones were posted to a ship registered in Malta, the SS *Tomerana*.

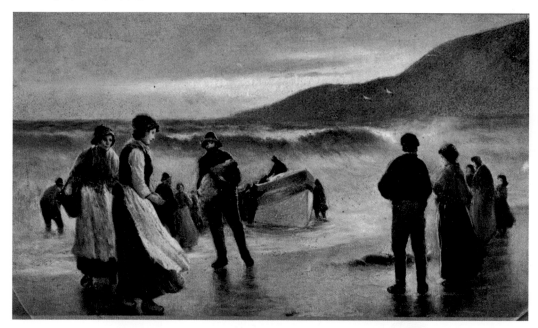